THE WELL-BALANCED SOUL

REWRITING

THE STORY OF

HUMAN NATURE

ADAM CARNEY

Printed in the United States of America
ISBN: 979-8-9956351-0-9
Published by: Integrative Psychology Publishing

ABOUT THE AUTHOR

Adam Carney is a writer, philosopher, and entrepreneur. He is the founder of Integrative Psychology, a psychology college in the United States. When he was 20, he left the United States to study yoga and Buddhism in India and returned forever changed. In 2018, he founded East+West, which quickly became one of the largest yoga schools in the world. He is now the youngest sitting president of a higher education institute in the US.

Contents

Part 1:

Part 2:

Part 3:

Part 4:

Introduction

"You cannot free yourself from chains you don't realize you are wearing."

-Franz Kafka

There are some stories that defy all logic, they should not happen and make no sense. Yet, they reach into some untouched chamber of the heart to unlock a hidden key you did not know was there.

Kōbun Chino Roshi was a Zen Buddhist teacher, born in 1938 in Niigata, Japan. The youngest of six children, he grew up surrounded by war and famine, often forced to eat pumpkin stems for dinner. When he was 12, his father died of cancer, and with nowhere else to go, he decided to become a monk.

Kōbun was an unconventional monk. He often warned students against following in his footsteps; instead, he encouraged them to get married and have children. He himself eventually had five; three daughters and two sons. In 1967, he came to America to teach Zen Buddhism. Among his thousands of students was Steve Jobs, who credited him with shaping Apple's minimalist design philosophy. He even officiated Jobs wedding in 1991. But Kōbun's story would take a dark and unexpected turn.

In 2002, he was on vacation with his family in Switzerland when his five-year-old daughter, Maya, fell into a backyard pond. Without second thought, he dove in to save her. Friends heard the commotion and rushed to help them, but it was too late. Kōbun and his daughter both drowned.

His students were both devastated and confused when they heard the news. Devastated, because they had just lost their beloved spiritual mentor. Confused, because the pond was only a few feet deep. How could he have drowned in such a shallow pond? However, those who knew Kōbun knew exactly what happened: he took his own life to be with his daughter in death.

I first heard this story during a meditation class on February 1, 2010—Kōbun's birthday—from one of his disciples who was there when he died. She spoke slowly, tears falling, each word carrying the gravity of immense loss. I never met Kōbun, and I know almost nothing about him; I don't know whether he was tall or short, how he laughed, or the color of his voice. Yet I find myself thinking about him often. I wonder what it would be like to be him. I think about his all-consuming love for his daughter, something I hope to know one day. I think about his courage and, in that mysterious act, perhaps, a glimpse into some unseen realm.

Kōbun and his story occupy a unique space in my heart, alongside many others, stories of men and women in history who sent ripples across time, stories that outlive their physical bodies and endure beyond even the rise and fall of civilizations. Too often, we try to understand history through events: who conquered whom, who ruled, who fell. But beneath this runs another history, a ***psychological and spiritual history***, more delicate, more enduring, and in the end more important. It lives through stories shared at dinner tables, in churches, and in yoga classes, and sometimes through tearful memories. It's the history of how we understand ourselves and how we make meaning of being alive. Carl Jung called it the "collective unconscious," a great cosmic river flowing through all of us. Some currents we all touch—figures like Freud, Jesus, Gandhi, the lives which redrew the map of thought. But there are countless others, too, quieter streams on the outskirts, whose influence is less visible but just as important. They touch us without meeting us, reminding us that something essential lies beyond the world we see.

Time has a way of distorting history, and the collective unconscious distorts with it. The distortion doesn't happen all at once but slowly, the way disease moves through a forest. Certain things get forgotten. Others become cemented. The poison spreads wide. It shapes how we see the world and how we understand ourselves, it shapes what we do and how we think, and hardly anyone notices. This book is a retelling of the story of human nature, how we understand ourselves, and a revision of an important thread in the collective unconscious, a thread that has distorted with time. For 2,400 years, I believe we've misunderstood something about ourselves, something vital, which has created a deep existential confusion in all of us. Confusion is not a feature of life; it's a disease.

REDUCTIONISM

Beneath the curve of the skull is the most mysterious object, a three-pound kingdom that was, for centuries, shrouded in myth. Today, through neuroscience, we map the firing of neurons and decode the chemistry of thoughts. Our technical understanding of the brain is remarkable. The paradox, however, is that it's rare to meet anyone who's happy. Our souls suffer more than ever, and spiritual poverty is normal. Psychology helps us understand ourselves, but it has become increasingly esoteric; it hardly even passes for a cohesive field of study anymore.

I must ask: What does it *actually* mean to be "complex"? From one standpoint, a garden is complex. You could spend your entire life dissecting a single rose. You could study the cells in each leaf and, further down, a single molecule. You could lose yourself in a single atom and never understand what a 'garden' actually is. The term for this is "reductionism," the belief that the best way to understand something is to break it into its smallest parts. Since the invention of the microscope in 1590, we've been addicted to reductionism, deeming anything else unreliable.

However, whether something is complex or simple depends on your *vantage point*. It's one thing to break a garden into infinitely divisible parts. It's another thing altogether to focus on *how to make your garden flourish*. To focus there, to tune out details and tend to what truly matters, is its own type of intelligence. There's a term for this as well: Wisdom.

To truly understand a garden, you must start with the basics: What's its purpose? What harms it? What makes it thrive?

One idea can change the world. It has happened before, and it can happen again. Newton, Darwin, and Einstein altered our grain of reality and revealed profound truths now obvious in hindsight. The Well-Balanced Soul is a profound truth, a central organizing principle for mental health. Once you see it, you can't unsee it. Like all universal truths, it is self-evident.

The principle is so simple that it can be stated in a single sentence. Seeing it is not the difficult part. The difficult part, as Franz Kafka once said, is that you can't free yourself from chains you don't realize you're wearing. The chains he's talking about are the patterns of the unconscious mind. The importance of any good idea is not how it is understood, but rather how it is lived. Before we can live with a Balanced Soul, we have to break those chains. And to break them, we need to understand where they came from, when they were forged, and why we accepted them. That's the work of this book. It's harder than you'd expect, and worth more than I can tell you. We'll move through crossroads in the collective unconscious, following stories that seem unrelated at first but start to build on each other as you go. I've threaded in pieces of my own journey throughout — how I came to know the Well-Balanced Soul from the inside.

This is not a self-help book or a collection of data but an intimate journey through the lives that have shaped us. We'll wander the streets of ancient Athens and sit with mystics from India. It's my love letter to the philosophers and spiritual teachers who have lit up my life in times of darkness. Like any real romance, it's messy—a mix of admiration and regret. You'll meet the people behind the ideas and come to know them as friends, flaws and all. No ideas are above revision, and I will challenge many of history's greatest thinkers. This book fills crucial gaps in psychology and builds a bridge to something truly new.

Wisdom is a spirit living inside you. Finding it is like discovering a trail of breadcrumbs God left for you. I have something urgent to say to you, and I wish to say it as if I were standing right there in the room with you: You are meant to be happy. But that is not a birthright. Happiness must be studied, cultivated, and worked for. To reach it, we must break chains and reimagine life itself.

15

Part One:

The Ancient Roots of the Mind

Making Music: Principles

There's no 'wrong' way to live, just as there's no wrong music. Different songs are for different occasions.

Some moments call for an uplifting song. Others call for something deeper and more sincere.

Both are beautiful in the right moment.

However, while no music is 'wrong,' not all music is pleasant. Music has principles: harmony, melody, and rhythm.

A thriving soul must start by learning principles.

Journal:

August 25, 1990: 6:04 PM.

My name is Adam. I was born in Elmhurst, Illinois, outside Chicago. A family of Italian, Irish, and Polish immigrants. A cuspy Virgo. My grandparents are first and second-generation Americans who grew up in poverty on the south side of Chicago. On my mother's side, my Polish grandfather sold windows and is a world-class casual investor. My grandmother is Italian, an administrator for the Mental Health Association in Waukesha County, Wisconsin.

On my father's side, my grandfather, fully Irish, 6'4 ", thin of frame, was a WWII vet, a devout Christian, and an entrepreneur. In the 1960s, he installed the first air conditioners in downtown Chicago skyscrapers. He became wealthy later in life and attended church every day. He loved playing the pipe organ; before he died, he donated $250,000 to his church to buy a new one. His wife, Eileen, was also Irish and a stay-at-home mom who raised my father and his two siblings. My father is a retired therapist—an LMFT who logged over 35,000 hours in his career. My mother studied business in college and worked as a sales rep for Eli Lilly before starting a consulting business, which she still runs today.

Nothing in my upbringing would suggest what happens in my life.

Journal: College

High school is like an American movie. Rated top in the nation in math and science. Friday night football games.

I study marketing in college.

Freshman year. I join a frat, then quickly drop out.

I take a class in Greek Philosophy. The professor is very old and wears tweed suits. For homework, he assigns Plato's Republic.

Science of the Soul: 1

Circa 405 BCE.

The city of Athens is tense. The greatest democracy the world has ever known lies broken, recently defeated by Sparta in the Peloponnesian War. The scorching, dry air of the marketplace hums with chatter as people gather to hear political speeches. The city that birthed philosophy, theater, and democracy now crawls with spies.

A strange man walks barefoot through the market. He's out of place; he's old, filthy, and unpleasant to look at. His face is weathered by years of poverty, and his clothes barely cover his frail body. Short, stocky, with a crooked nose and bulging eyes, historians say he resembles a satyr. He is known for his strange behavior, often stopping mid-conversation, standing motionless, lost in thought. The man's name is Socrates, son of Sophroniscus, a stonemason, and Phaenarete, a midwife. He had a habit of goading strangers into debate, often to the point of agitation. He targeted Athenian aristocrats and asked deep philosophical questions. Socrates claimed to be possessed by a 'spirit daimon' that guided all his actions. Yet, beneath his disheveled exterior was a spiritual magnetism that drew others to him. He exuded deep inner stillness and the mystical gravity of someone tuned into a mystical dimension.

Socrates should have died in obscurity. But fate has other plans.

Journal: I Am Lost

Sophomore year. I fall in love on vacation. Small town girl. "More cows than people." We spend a summer on her family's farm.

A simple life. I feel happy. I learn the magic of following my heart. Is this my future? Not quite. She cheats. I'm broken. Impermanence stings.

College loses its meaning. I am lost.

Science of the Soul: 2

In his youth, Socrates served as an Athenian soldier in the Peloponnesian War. He was a brave and respected fighter, but his comrades remembered him for his unusual behavior: marching barefoot in the snow and going days without food. He had a rare gift: a superhuman endurance, which he used to explore life's deepest questions. His mind was rigorous, his focus relentless, and his gaze was often fixed on the most important question: What makes a good life?

He believed the answer to this question already exists in every person, but that it is buried under layers of social conditioning. His job was to help others "give birth" to their innate wisdom through deep questioning. He referred to himself as a "Midwife of the Soul."

The Socratic Method

We see Socrates process most clearly in the dialogue *Gorgias*. In a famous scene, Socrates arrives late to a party of Athenian aristocrats at the home of Callicles, a hedonistic socialite and politician. Callicles is drunk and surrounded by women. Socrates prompts a philosophical inquiry.

> **Socrates:** *"Dear Callicles, tell us about your way of life, and why we should follow it."*

Callicles takes the bait.

> **Callicles:** *"Moderation teaches people to suppress their desires. That is for children! The truth is this: freedom and luxury are the sources of virtue. Everything else is just pretty words that go against nature."*

Step 1: Find the Principle.

The Socratic Method starts with simple questions. Obvious ones. Questions that shouldn't be hard to answer — and that's exactly the point. The simplicity draws out a person's real principles. It's a Rorschach test disguised as small talk.

> **Socrates:** *"Callicles, it sounds like you are saying a good life comes from being able to satisfy your desires. Is this correct?"*

> **Callicles:** *"More or less, yes that is what I'm saying."*

Inquisitive neutrality is key to the Socratic Method. Socrates' humility was legendary. Every conversation is pure exploration.

Socrates: *"Imagine a person who can never satisfy their thirst. Would this person be happy?"*

Callicles: *"Of course not. Such a person would live like a stone."*

Socrates: *"And what if someone is always thirsty but always has water to drink? Would this person live a better life than someone with moderate thirst?"*

Callicles: *"You're being ridiculous, Socrates."*

Socrates: *"I'm following your logic. Your premise is that happiness is derived from being free and able to satisfy all your desires. So wouldn't the person with intense thirst, who could always satisfy it, be the happiest? Is the person with the most intense desires, who can satisfy them all, the happiest?"*

Step 2: The Stress Test.

This is where the method gets interesting. The stress test involves pushing a principle to its logical extreme. Socrates takes Callicles' principle that "satisfying desires is the key to a good life," and puts it to the ultimate test.

This is the most overlooked step of the Socratic method. Why is it so important? Because good principles are *very* subtle. Socrates once said that getting to the truth of deep moral questions is like trying to read a book from a mile away. The text is too small to read. To understand it, he said we must "enlarge" the logical principle by projecting it onto a mountain nearby. By examining the logical extremes, we can better see the nuances of the principle. That's what he's doing here with Callicles.

Step 3: Make Distinctions.

He goes on.

> **Socrates:** *"Are all pleasures equally good? Is the pleasure of drinking wine the same as the pleasure of receiving wisdom? Some desires, when fulfilled, leave us wanting more. Others bring lasting contentment. Surely these differences matter?"*

This is how Socrates works. Precise. Methodical. Socrates is a reductionist. The goal of his method isn't to win an argument — it's to make **distinctions** between things we've lazily grouped under the same word. At first, the distinctions seem minor. Trivial even. They aren't. They're the distinctions that run our entire lives. They are part of the core programming of the unconscious mind. For example, we have one word for "pleasure," but Socrates uncovers a critical distinction between pleasure that fills the soul and pleasure that drains it. There's pleasure in eating ice cream, but ice cream makes us gain weight and feel sluggish on the back end. There's also pleasure in playing music, but music doesn't have the same sort of hangover. These small distinctions matter—they are the entire point of the Socratic method. They allow us to see life more clearly and make better decisions that create harmony in the soul. He believed that when we overlook these distinctions, our lives fall off course.

By the end of the conversation, Callicles falls silent. His certainty is shaken. He's not convinced, but he reaches a state the Greeks called "Aporia"—a productive confusion where you realize your old definitions don't work. Aporia creates openness for new information to flood in. Most people avoid this feeling. Socrates embraced it.

> *"We must first empty the mind of weeds before anything new can grow."*

The Gorgias is a masterclass on the virtue of moderation, a central tenet of Socratic Ethics. It highlights the crucial distinction between insatiable, addictive desires that trap us and noble desires that nourish the soul. Moderation isn't just about "eating less," it's a state of spiritual maintenance and the most essential habit in the pursuit of happiness. It's the wisdom of knowing it's healthy to take *less*. An abundance of the wrong pleasures can quickly degrade the soul, trapping it in cycles of seeking that can't be filled. A soul that knows moderation is a soul that can live in a world surrounded by addictive traps and still maintain integrity. A woman in the market once asked Socrates why, if he had renounced all possessions, he spent so much time in the marketplace.

"To remind me of all the things I am free from."

The Greeks described this state using the word sophrosyne (σωφροσύνη), or 'soundness of mind.' Marcus Aurelius, who studied the Socratic Method extensively, later cited it as the cornerstone of Stoic Philosophy.

Socrates' reputation grew in Athens. Many of his followers grew impatient with his painstaking questioning, wanting him to cut to the chase and plainly share his principles with them. He never obliged. He knew that giving his students answers bypassed the important process of discovering them for themselves. The fruit is not in definitions, but in the process of picking out the mind's weeds one by one, discarding social conditioning. The Socratic Method is not about reaching a destination. It's a process for developing clear, virtuous inner principles that truly improve life. What is virtue? What is beauty? What is justice? We use these words every day, yet we don't really understand them, so we keep cycling through the same issues. We don't evolve because we live with vague principles that unconsciously control us.

Can you objectively define what makes a good life? Most people would say no; life is subjective. Socrates disagreed. He believed there are objective foundations to a good life; however, they are subtle, and you must dig to find them. That's why the Socratic Method is so powerful.

Reading Socrates is dense. At times, your brain will hurt. But the reward is an undeniable feeling that you are gaining something rare and precious, and becoming a better person. No one who has ever seen the world through Socrates' eyes can ever unsee it.

Journal: Leaving The Path

2011: Oahu, Hawaii.

I'm on a hotel balcony in Waikiki. I see a strange gold tower in the lush mountainside in the distance. I take a bus.

It's a Buddhist temple. I meet a monk who wears Crocs and hits plastic golf balls off the mountain.

I visit weekly. He gives me a green paper booklet with a Tibetan prayer inside. I do it every day for a year.

Something begins to awaken inside me. I feel bliss for no reason. My inner world vibrates with joy. I extend my trip.

I'm on a stand-up paddle. A sudden wave of bliss washes through me. Shivers through the spine. This is new.

A deep voice tells me to drop out of college and leave home forever. I listen.

What is Beauty?

Beauty. We see it in waterfalls and paintings and people. It's one of Socrates' favorite topics. Can we define it? In another famous scene in the book *Phaedrus*, Socrates searches for the answer to this question as he walks through the marketplace with a young man named Phaedrus.

"This vase is beautiful; shall I buy it?" Phaedrus asks.

"Indeed," Socrates replies. "But tell me, what makes it beautiful?"

"Well, its proportions, its colors, the way it catches the light," says Phaedrus.

"Ah, so you're saying that beauty lies in these visible qualities?" replies Socrates.

"Yes, exactly."

Socrates stops to ponder. "Could you define beauty?"

Phaedrus takes a long pause and goes blank. "I cannot."

"It is unwise," Socrates warns, "to speak of beauty without questioning its source. If beauty is what you see with your eyes, then why do we also call a piece of music beautiful? Or a waterfall? Or an act of courage? None of these things has visible properties. Is the source of beauty really in what is visible? You say this vase is beautiful because of its proportions and colors. But surely you've seen other vases with different proportions and different colors that you also found beautiful. So beauty, by definition, cannot be this particular combination of visible qualities, can it? When you look at this vase and call it beautiful, your soul is recognizing something it already knows. It reminds your soul of something in the higher spiritual realms—the eternal pattern of Beauty. "

Initially, this may sound like another pedantic conversation, but this reveals a psychological tendency that's easy to overlook. To Socrates, "beauty" is a latent memory that's imprinted and stored in the mind. It's like an old memory from a previous life we've forgotten. Beauty is not in the material world; it is the memory of a higher realm stored inside us. The illusion is that beauty lies outside us, in objects. The true source of beauty is not in external objects but the latent memory of a higher realm. Why is this important? Because if you believe beauty is "out there," you'll continually search for something "out there." When you understand that the true source of beauty is inside you, you no longer need to seek anything outside yourself. The same goes for virtue, justice, and anything we innately sense has "goodness" in it. They are subtle memories inside the soul of what the higher realm is like.

Socrates' students would later describe these latent memories as "Forms," patterns imprinted in the unconscious and evoked by external experiences. They are essential to understanding Socrates' world, and the reason Socrates emphasizes self-study above all else.

Socrates never wrote a single word, and if it weren't for a chance encounter with a well-born teenager, we'd have no record of him.

Science of the Soul: 3

"I met a man today who showed me that everything I know is built on sand."

-Plato

Greece, 407 BCE.

It happens by chance at the gym. In Athens, gyms weren't just for exercise; they were sprawling complexes of colonnades and gardens that were schools, social clubs, and political forums all in one. Socrates is doing what he does: goading strangers into debate. On this day, he runs into someone he did not expect.

The young man's name was Aristocles, though you likely know him by his nickname—Plato, meaning "broad," given to him perhaps for his broad intellect, or maybe his famously wide shoulders. Plato was around twenty years old, born into one of Athens' most prominent families. His stepfather,

Pyrilampes, was a close friend of the famous orator Pericles, one of the grandfathers of democracy. His mother, Perictione, was the daughter of Solon, a famous statesman who history would remember as the man who abolished debt slavery. The gym was one of Socrates' favorite places to dialogue. He particularly enjoyed dialoguing with young aristocratic men like Plato, who were intellectually rigorous without the calcification of mind that often accompanies old age.

Politics was in Plato's DNA. Everything in his upbringing suggested he would follow the path of a statesman. But Plato was not like other young men. He was shy, particularly drawn to theater, and more interested in poetry than politics. From a young age, he read Homer and was a remarkably talented playwright. According to the ancient biographer Diogenes Laertius, he was one of the most promising young artists of his generation, his verses displaying a rare combination of technical skill and emotional depth.

Their conversation lasted hours. Some accounts suggest it lasted days. Socrates used his usual method, asking simple questions relentlessly, but something was different this time. Most people got frustrated with Socrates' questioning and left. Plato keeps going. He senses Socrates hold mysterious wisdom and wants to discover what it is.

When Plato finally returned home, he reportedly said to his family, "I met a man today who showed me that everything I know is built on sand."

He gathered all his poetry and burned it.

Censoring Artists

It was not coincidence that Plato burned his poetry after meeting Socrates. One of Socrates' most controversial ideas was that he advocated for the strict censorship of art and poetry. Art, he observed, has tremendous power over the human mind and soul. It shapes how people (particularly young people) see the world. Stories shape minds in a process that is difficult to reverse.

Most Greeks in the time of Socrates were educated primarily through Homer's epics *The Iliad* and *The Odyssey*. Socrates despised Homer. He believed his books programmed an entire generation to worship power and hedonism. Homer portrayed gods as vengeful and deceptive, swayed by the same petty issues that trouble humans. Zeus tricks mortals, Ares is a warmonger, and Aphrodite seduces men. Socrates believed these stories brainwashed Greeks into believing the universe is working against them, and that there isn't a more virtuous higher realm. He often spoke about the unimaginable damage this caused to the psyche of his countrymen. Homer's stories were entertaining but soured the souls of readers. A young person who grew up reading Homer learned that deception and violence are justified, when in the name of glory. These aren't values that create a harmonious society. Socrates believed in censoring art because artists didn't understand their influence; they don't consider the consequences their work has on delicate unconscious minds. Poets write about love without understanding the nuances between love and lust. Painters create works about courage without understanding the distinctions between courage and recklessness. Art has the power to shape souls, and if artists weren't educated in ethics, they could unintentionally damage minds for generations. His solution was that all youth should be required to go through ethical training to learn the Forms of Virtue, Justice, and Beauty before they are allowed to create art.

As an artist, I wrestle with this. My first instinct is to reject the idea entirely. It feels draconian. But Socrates forced me to ask harder questions of myself. Every year, I watch the collective unconscious degrade and become more poisoned by media that ignores its impact on mental health. Most art today is designed to unapologetically suck attention, unaware of the downstream effects it might have. Movies that glorify greed and vice and normalize abuse. The effects on us are not obvious, but nothing in the unconscious mind is. I now distinguish between two very different types of art. There's work I create to process my own darkness. It's necessary and cathartic. It helps me understand myself. And then there's the work I create to try to improve the world—pieces for beauty intended to uplift and create a positive experience for others. Both are valuable. But Socrates would ask: Do they serve the same purpose? Should they be shared and consumed equally? I've landed on something that feels true: I create both, but I only share or sell Art I genuinely believe will improve the lives of others. The art I share publicly, I try to create with awareness of its effect—not to diminish its honesty, but to ensure I'm not using my creative power for selfish attention-seeking. The resolution is not censorship. It's discernment. It's the kind of internal regulation Socrates called for— deeper awareness of how we live and how that might affect the fragile psyche. The question isn't "Can I create this?" but "What is the full impact of this?"

Socrates made me stop defending the assumption that all art, regardless of its intent or impact, deserves uncritical celebration. Some art elevates. Some art degrades. Pretending otherwise is cowardice.

Science of the Soul: 4

Plato begins following Socrates everywhere. He starts to understand that Socrates homeless appearance is deceiving, a clever bit of cosmic theatre used to disarm others. He sees a deeply spiritual man embodying a disciplined life that prioritizes the soul's development. Socrates' "spirit daimon" that drove him was not psychosis but a channel to a spirit from another realm. It wasn't a coincidence that miracles happened around him constantly.

One afternoon, Plato and Socrates are walking through the market when they come across a boy sitting alone, crying, his face buried in his hands. He had been caught stealing bread. Socrates sits beside him attentively without saying a word. When the boy finally looks up, Socrates unexpectedly asks: "What do you dream of for your life?" The question catches him off guard. They talk until sunset, and Socrates never mentions the crime. Instead, he speaks about what it means for the soul to be hungry—not for food, but for dignity, purpose, and a life that matters. When they stand to leave, the boy is weeping. His life is changed forever. Socrates sat with prostitutes, traumatized soldiers, and wealthy men alike, treating each with dignity, as if they were the most important person in the world. Teaching was a high-paying profession in Athens, and people often insisted on paying him, but Socrates refused payment.

It's entirely through Plato's books that we know Socrates. It's disputed by historians whether the Socrates we know as the High King of Philosophy is the Socrates of truthful account or filtered through the lens of Plato's brilliant mind. Personally, I don't care. I'm not a reductionist.

In his dialogues, including *The Republic, The Symposium, Phaedo, and Apology*, which have been read and cited by leaders throughout history, Plato married his poetic gifts with his love of the Socratic Method, creating an entirely new literary form. It's equal parts self-development, spiritual inquiry, and political debate —the birth of Philosophy.

Plato characterizes Socrates as both full of flaws and touched by the divine, who uses his piercing intellect in selfless service to his students' spiritual growth. His books are philosophical theater, true masterpieces of craft and poetry, where complex ideas come alive through the interplay of characters. Each scene is crafted like a beautiful symphony, establishing a central philosophical theme that grows in intricacy. The dialogues are packed with deep, precious bits of wisdom:

People who live moderately are more content than those who indulge every pleasure.

People who are honest have less anxiety and sleep more peacefully.

Children whose education nurtures both their physical bodies and who study the arts are the most virtuous later in life.

Justice is not an individual act, but a society where people develop excellence of craft and stay within the limits of their excellence.

Those who regularly examine their motivations and principles live with greater coherence between their stated values and actual behavior.

The deepest friendships form not through shared pleasures but through mutual pursuit of excellence and truth.

The person who acts unjustly damages their own soul more severely than any harm they inflict on their victim.

"Beauty" is any experience that brings us into higher realms of thought.

These are only a small appetizer of Plato's insights. He envisioned a world where every child learns the Socratic Method. Why study speech if you don't know how to speak virtuously? Why learn engineering if it's not in service to a higher good? Why become a leader if you don't understand justice?

PRINCIPLES FOR THE SOUL

To Plato, the great tragedy of human life was that we spend enormous energy on things that don't satisfy the soul, while ignoring the pursuits that will. We chase pleasure, addictions, and material success, despite the way they degrade our soul. Platonic philosophy is the pursuit of principles for living that satisfy the soul. A principle is a fundamental truth that acts as the foundation for a system of belief, behavior, or a chain of reasoning. Plato believed that just as there are laws governing the health of the body, there are laws governing the health of the soul. He rejects the notion that happiness is subjective. The principles of good living are as precise and discoverable as Pythagoras's mathematics, a "Science of the Soul," the source code governing our thoughts, habits, and futures. Every honest attempt we make to discover them improves our lives dramatically.

Gandhi once said, "Your actions express your priorities," meaning that our principles are displayed by the way we live. To Plato, the purpose of principles was not to win debates but to demonstrate them through consistent actions which lead to a better life, and better society. He lived a disciplined life of moderation and spiritual development, often to extremes. He never married or pursued positions of influence. He devoted his entire life to educating others through his academy. His ideas were powerful because he demonstrated them.

Plato introduced the vision of a society governed by principles instead of the whims of monarchs. It's difficult to overstate how dramatically this has transformed the world across time. Today, we take for granted that society operates under rationally developed principles. We debate policy changes that maximize good and minimize harm. Courts reference precedent. Constitutional rights protect citizens from arbitrary authority. This is done imperfectly, of course, but the notion that society is best governed by principles (rather than whims) is deeply embedded in the Western psyche. It's obvious now. This wasn't obvious then.

It was universally believed in Plato's time that anyone who ascended to power did so because God favored them. Every few years, new leaders assumed power with different visions, and society was redesigned to suit them. If a regime valued a certain religion, it restructured society around that. If they wanted new laws, they would write them. There was no foundation and no shared agreement about what made a society work. People lived at the mercy of whoever held power. If a leader didn't like you, there was no principle protecting you. Society was a ship constantly changing course based on whoever grabbed the wheel.

Plato saw that society would never evolve unless we began studying and documenting reality to extract principles that maximize good and minimize harm. Proper governing principles are not handed down by gods or monarchs; they should be discovered through observation and reason. This formed the psychological underpinning that allowed the creation of democracy. He knew this could only happen if everyone participated. Collaboration is an often-overlooked feature of the Socratic Method. Many of Plato's dialogues are four or five people in conversation, volleying complicated ideas back and forth, searching for better ideas. Socrates is often challenged and expands his perspective. Through hearing multiple perspectives, the collective perspective expands.

But not everyone loved Plato and Socrates. The power of principles is that they exist independently of any individual's preference. This threatened the fundamental basis of individual political power. If principles govern society, leaders can't do whatever they want. It regulates their whims and fantasies, and their right to subject others to them. Every time Socrates questioned someone's reasoning in public, he demonstrated that authority must justify itself through principles. Every time he revealed contradictions in a leader's thinking, he proved that principles matter more than "divine favor." He was showing humanity that living under arbitrary rule is not an inevitability. We can build society on foundations discovered through observing what's worked. Stable foundations regardless of who's in charge.

We take for granted the immense gift of living in a society governed by principles. These features are by no means obvious to the modern eye. Things like private property rights, independent courts, separation of powers, and due process. We forget these are still relatively new features of society, and that they are not naturally occurring— they're hard-won inventions through centuries of our ancestors' trial and error. We were born into a world where these already existed. You've never known a world where suddenly, a king can volunteer you as a human sacrifice to the gods and get away with it. Yes, our systems are imperfect, but it's easy to feign gratitude for how much we've inherited when it's all we know. Ironically, today, not only do we overlook this immense gift, but we also often demonize it. Yes, culture is formed by art, music, and language. But it's also formed by principles, reasoned through by our ancestors, so we do not repeat mistakes of the past. It's easy to overlook this gift— something so ubiquitous we forget to notice it.

After Greece, principle-led societies keep losing to monarchies. Rome—still heavily influenced by the Greeks— had periods of republic but would always gravitate back to the rule of kings. Someone would organize society around law and reason. It would work for a while, then collapse back. A new strong man, a new dynasty. That is, until America.

In 1776, only five small republics existed in the entire world—Venice, Genoa, San Marino, the Dutch Republic, and a handful of tiny Italian city-states, together representing less than 1% of the world's population. Democracy was purely theoretical; there were so many historical failures that the prevailing belief was that it could never be done. America was the first to break this cycle permanently at scale. The founders built a system to prevent any individual from becoming more powerful than the principles of law. Almost all the founding fathers, particularly James Madison, Thomas Jefferson, John Adams, and Alexander Hamilton, studied Plato's dialogues extensively. They proved rational government was possible. In a way, they were the first to realize Plato's vision. Once demonstrated, the idea spread. Two hundred years later, roughly half the world's population lived in nations with democratic foundations.

It's important to be critical of how we're governed. The level of disagreement in our world today can at times, feel like a burden. However, the most peaceful times in history aren't when one party is firmly in power—ironically, they're in times of muddled government. Conflict and debate aren't a bug of a functioning society but a feature. The presence of visible conflict is evidence that we have principles to debate and the freedom to debate them. That process can feel challenging when you're in it, but it's only possible in a society built on principles. We critique our world the way we critique at our family—hyper-sensitive to the flaws. But healing means acknowledging strengths, too, and we overlook them precisely because we're so accustomed to them. Many societies today still live without the foundations of objective principles, which is exactly why they can't evolve—they remain subject to the whims of whoever's in power. Laws and principles are less sexy than art, but just as important to culture.

All of this begins with Socrates and Plato. The freedom to question authority through reason. The commitment to discovering better ideas through honest observation. The willingness to admit when something isn't working and try something new. Looking at our world now, it's easy to see the flaws and want to tear it down. Our principles are flawed. They favor some over others. They evolve slowly. But that all rests on the foundation of distilled agreements of thousands of years of our ancestors' trial and error. The right to a fair trial emerged from centuries of people being executed without evidence. Property rights evolved from the observation that humans have a greater incentive to care for and maintain what they own. Free markets and speech emerged as a buffer against centralized power. Police forces ensure we don't suddenly revert to our tendency toward violence, which humans tend to do if not governed. These laws didn't come from kings. They're bottom-up agreements, hard-won principles about what creates stable societies. We live in a world where power typically changes hands without violence. That's still new in human history. Our society isn't perfect. But framed against the full scope of history, we're extraordinarily lucky to inherit it. Plato envisioned a society where reason governed rather than force or bloodline. We live in a version of that society—flawed, but in many ways real. This is Socrates and Plato's legacy—a society built on principles and the reliance on reason rather than force.

But they didn't just democratize political principles. They gave us something even more fundamental. Before Socrates, God was mediated entirely through those in power. Kings ruled because God favored them. The only way to understand virtue was to subject yourself to those "chosen" by God to be in power. Socrates shatters this. He demonstrates that anyone—a stonemason, a prostitute, a slave—could use reason to discover virtue. He insisted on owning nothing to prove that this is possible for literally anyone. He taught us not to seek answers through powerful, impressive figures, but instead to seek them through self-study. Discover wisdom for yourself. Socrates and Plato democratized *access to God.*

I've lived periods without clear life principles. No rules, just following pleasure wherever it leads. The "freedom" feels good for a time. But I always return to craving something larger. Chasing pleasure and status is a momentary high that quickly fades, like food with no nutrition. Socrates is one of history's most underrated spiritual teachers and a role model for anyone seeking to support the spiritual development of others. Inner principles give structure to what we accept and reject. They help us thrive over time. Without this inner foundation, addictive forces quickly overrun our lives, pulling us away from what truly makes us happy.

To this day, no one in history has covered this topic with such intricacy and precision. Plato and Socrates are some of the greatest contributors to improving the human condition. They hold keys we desperately need to remember about creating a good life and society. This is why you still know their names.

Journal: I Give Up

2013:

I'm 23. No money. I move to Santa Monica. I take a job in Venture Capital.

There's money everywhere. I help build companies I care nothing about. Parties in West Hollywood. I hate technology but I build it. I drink lots of Starbucks.

Meditation feels stiff. Something isn't working.

Outwardly I'm enthusiastic. Inwardly, repulsed by everything around me. I have more than I ever dreamed. Job, condo, friends. Something is deeply off.

I'm in a movie theater. What's happening? I'm scared. Panic attacks begin.

I can't sleep. I can't sit still. My mind cycles into pits of darkness. Unbearable pressure. Confusion. No help. Tortured from something I don't understand. Meditation makes it worse. Is this hell? The only thing that helps is drinking.

I'm in a bar. 'The Bungalow.' It's Tuesday. Beautiful people and a sunset. Kate Hudson is flirting with me at the bar. I'm out alone. Not because I want to be. It's the only alternative to panic attacks.

I break inside. I can't take this anymore. I close my eyes and say a prayer.

"I give up. Tell me what to do."

"Go to India," says a voice inside me.

The next morning I quit my job.

I book a flight.

And Now, Yoga

Circa 300 BCE, Northern India:

3,500 miles southeast of Athens, something else was developing that would profoundly influence the collective understanding of human nature. India under the Guptas was in a golden age — science, math, and the arts all moving at once. More interesting, though, was what was happening philosophically. Yoga, Buddhism, and Samkhya were in genuine dialogue for the first time. The borders between traditions were unusually porous. Ideas were moving.

A common practice in the ancient East was to never write down spiritual teachings. Buddhist, Taoist, and many Hindu teachings circulated orally for centuries after their founders lived. To a Western ear, this probably sounds odd. The reason is that the teachings were considered too alive to survive the page intact. Too dependent on the relationship between teacher and student, on human presence, and context. Writing, in their view, removes the living spirit. It locks the teaching in time, strips it of context, and kills it.

A man in northern India decides to break this tradition and begin documenting the Vedic spiritual practices of India. We don't know much about what Patanjali looks like. When depicted, he's usually sitting in meditation, eyes cast downward in full lotus, his legs coiled together like a snake. What we do know is that Patanjali is one of India's great geniuses with a remarkable intellect and deep spiritual wisdom. He's a unique combination of spiritual master, scientist, and poet. At the time, yoga was esoteric, practiced only in Ashrams outside cities. Patanjali felt it was finally time someone write down the scattered methods to make them more accessible to the common man. Patanjali didn't invent yoga. According to tradition, yoga was invented by the god Shiva, who taught yoga to humans to help them maintain a connection to nature and God. Yoga had been practiced for thousands of years before Patanjali, well into prehistory. He was the first to gather the scattered oral teachings and organize them into a codified collection of instructions, which Yogis throughout history acknowledge as the bible of yogic practice. It's called the Yoga Sutras. It begins like this:

Verse 1: Atha yoga-anushasanam. "And now, Yoga is Presented."

It's said Patanjali chose the words, "And now, Yoga," because he's speaking to the common people living in cities.

As if to say, "And now that you've realized the external world is unsatisfying and illusory, it's time to go inward and learn yoga." It's said that anyone who begins practicing yoga is at an important stage in their spiritual evolution.

Verse 2: Yoga chitta vritti nirodhah. "Yoga is the stilling of the changing states of the mind."

This is the mission statement, the distilled essence of yoga in a single sentence. Pause for a moment and notice where your attention is right now. You might be thinking about what you need to do later. Or replaying a conversation from yesterday. Your body is here. Your mind is somewhere else entirely. Next, pause and notice exactly what's in the physical space around you. The temperature of the air. Sounds in the distance. The light hitting the floor. See the gap? You probably weren't contemplating the feeling of the ground under your feet, or the color of the walls, or the subtle smells circulating. You were thinking about something that already happened or something that might happen later. We live in our heads, not in reality. This is what yogis mean by "illusion." It's not that your thoughts are fake—they are real because you experience them — but they're almost never about what's actually happening.

According to Patanjali, we can't begin living in reality until we recognize this endless stream of mental chatter. The mind is basically a sophisticated sorting machine. It takes the vast universe and chops it into pieces: this is "me," that's "you," this happened "then," that might happen "later." Super useful in some situations. But the problem with this is that the boundaries we create don't exist outside our minds. We get so good at this chopping and sorting that we forget it's not actually happening. Yogis call this mental division "chitta." While chitta is useful, if we over-rely on it, we get addicted to living in our heads. We forget there's a whole dimension of reality happening *right now* that has nothing to do with our chopping and sorting.

When I first read the sutras, I had no idea what they were talking about. "Stilling the changing states of the mind" felt like a different language.

FROM THE INSIDE

Had I never gone to India, I would have never believed this was possible. What Patanjali doesn't mention here is that the key to stilling the mind is to train the *feeling sense*. Feeling and thinking are mutually exclusive — you can't think and feel at the same time. The more you think, the less you feel, and the more you feel, the less you think. Many people try to "stop thinking," but quickly realize it's simply not possible. The key to reducing overthinking is to move energy through your

body to activate the feeling sense. Yogis say there are "energy channels" that need to be awakened through practices like breath and movement — "knocking on the pipes from the outside," as if clearing a clogged gutter. It doesn't happen instantly. It's a neurological retraining that takes many years. But as you do, you'll feel your energy channels open and begin to experience new sensations in your body. Naturally, over time, the mind begins to pacify. Life opens up in a new way.

I went through this myself beginning in 2014, the first time I went to India. Prior to learning yoga, I was meditating every day but still living entirely in my mind. My body was closed, and I couldn't feel much. Yoga opened up an entirely new dimension of life — simpler, but more exciting because it's alive in a way the mind never is. It feels strange at first because we're trained in the West to believe that living in the mind protects us. I think of my life in two distinct categories: before India, and after.

Verse 3: Tada drashtuh svarupe vasthanam. "When you do, the practitioner abides in its true nature."

What we think of as "I" is not our true nature. It's a trick the mind plays on us. The true nature of "I" is much more vast, connected, and mysterious, a continuous process that includes every person and every experience that's ever shaped you. That's not something the logical, chopping/sorting mind can grasp.

The more we engage the felt sense by moving energy through the body, the less we live in illusions of the mind, and the more we can live in *actual reality*. The more we live in reality, the more we understand the spiritual dimension, and the true nature of being alive. That's the map of Patanjali's yoga sutras. They bear little resemblance to what we practice today. Most people would find it impossibly rigorous. There's no mention of specific yoga poses—most of those come centuries later. Patanjali's yoga is a whole-life transformation system with eight sequential stages, and you don't get to skip ahead.

1. Moral restraints (yamas)
2. Positive observances (niyamas)
3. Physical postures (asana)
4. Breath expansion (pranayama)
5. Withdrawal of the senses (pratyahara)
6. Concentration (dharana)
7. Meditation (dhyana)
8. Samadhi (blissful living)

The Sutras are a detailed instruction manual for deep spiritual connection. They have been translated more times than almost any non-religious text in history — first into Persian at the request of a Mughal emperor, later into German by Romantic philosophers searching for an antidote to Cartesian rationalism, and most recently in neuroscience labs, where researchers keep arriving at conclusions Patanjali wrote down in 400 CE.

CONTRADICTIONS

But there's a big problem with this. Like Socrates, yogis believe the purpose of life is finding connection with a higher realm of consciousness. Socrates says you get there through clear principles discovered only through the *rational mind*. Yogis say that spiritual connection begins only when we *stop thinking* altogether; that *thinking itself* eliminates the possibility of finding it. They agree on the goal, but the two approaches could not be more different. Socrates says, "Think your way to truth." Patanjali says, "Thinking is the problem."

So, which is it?

Journal: The Cold Part of India

October 4, 2013. Dharamsala, India.

5:30 AM. I wake up and it's 35°F. A single bed (wood plank?). Empty concrete room. I didn't know Dharamshala was in the mountains. I didn't know India got this cold. 15 seconds of hot water. I'm wearing the only two sweatshirts I brought.

I enter the yoga room. 35-day training in Hatha Yoga. Every day a unique struggle. Feels like I'm in jail. For some reason, I'm getting happier.

I see the Dalai Lama speak in his home temple. He flees here in 1959 and takes most of Tibet with him. He walks in the room and monks bow and cry. I cry too.

I sit in a vegan cafe and see a man in a turban whose presence reminds me of Rafiki from The Lion King. I know instantly he's the one I came to India to meet.

I come to India with questions.

I want answers.

Some people are born with physical deformities—legs, or arms, or ears missing. And some are born with less visible deformities of the mind or spirit or character. Hidden, but no less crippling.

I was born this way, as I hadn't felt God in my life until that day. Every crevice of me drenched in suffering. When you're born with something missing, you never question it because it's never been there. A world without wonder and real love was normal to me. Naturally, I assumed everyone lived this way.

I don't remember anything he said.
I'll never forget how it felt to be around him.
He loved me and I loved him.
I wanted answers. He shows me presence instead.
My questions no longer mattered. Hand to heart, this man gave me an arm I was never meant to have.

"What do I do now?"
"Enjoy your life!" he laughs.

Science of the Soul: 5

Later in his life, Plato turns his attention to his greatest challenge: mapping the human soul.

This was a gargantuan task. Plato initially struggled, finding that every definition revealed new holes he hadn't seen before. He studied the thinkers who came before him, yet their descriptions all felt partial— like paintings of a mountain showing only one side. His breakthrough came when he realized that the "self" is not a single entity, but a living collaboration of *three distinct forces*. The soul is multidimensional, made of systems that think, systems of emotional responses, and a raw, animalistic urge. To bring this to life, Plato gave us one of history's most enduring metaphors: The Tripartite Chariot. He invites us to imagine the human soul as a chariot made up of three entities:

1. The Chariot Driver: Logic and Intellect

The chariot driver represents the intellect. His duty is to plot a course and navigate. He scans the horizon, identifies patterns, and chooses a direction. The chariot is the part of us that forms and contemplates principles to live by. However, the driver cannot actually move the system. That comes from the two horses.

2. The Noble, Well-Tamed Horse: Identity

This is our social identity—the version of ourselves we polish and present to gain respect and a sense of belonging. This is the source of our "high" emotions: courage, ambition, and honor. While noble, this horse can be vain; it cares deeply about how it's perceived by others. Its downfall is that it identifies with its own nobility, so it's also the center of emotional reactions—the part of us that flares up when our self-image is challenged.

3. The Wild, Untamed Horse: The Appetite

This is our animalistic instinct, wild, mysterious, and untamed. Strong, energetic, and with restless energy, the wild horse is often deaf to the driver's instructions. This represents primal urges: hunger, thirst, and sex.

Plato's Chariot is a remarkable insight that captures the nuance and complexity of human nature. We are made up of dynamic systems that, on one level, bear no resemblance to one another, yet on another level are deeply interconnected.

But Plato wasn't just describing the soul. His ambition was to discover the **single principle** that would allow anyone to live with a satisfied soul. An objective math formula for happiness.

He noticed that intellect separates us from other animals. It allows us to see beyond immediate gratification. The realm of reason, Plato argued, is closest to the divine, and we can only reach it through the chariot driver (logic) taking firm control. Problems arise when the hierarchy inverts. When the tamed horse takes over, we're consumed by pride and performative vanity. When the untamed horse leads, we become enslaved to cycles of pleasure seeking that can never be fulfilled. Only when the driver holds the reins, regulating the other two systems, can we truly have inner harmony. He called this the "Well-Ordered Soul."

Context here is important. Plato was speaking to a generation of corrupt political leaders in which power was indistinguishable from virtue. Men like Callicles the Hedonist, raised on Homer, who had little awareness of the concept of a soul. The strong do what they will, and that's nature's code. Into this world, Plato offered a radical proposition: the soul is happiest when the Chariot Driver—the rational intellect—firmly regulates the two horses. He was trying to prove to his contemporaries that neither power nor status would make them happy. This had never occurred to them. Why must the intellect lead? Because only rational thought can formulate virtuous inner principles and give us reason to escape the addictive cycles of lower urges. Only through intellect can we understand the Forms of Beauty, Courage, Justice, and Virtue. Without the intellect firmly leading, we endlessly seek pleasure, power, and status, which can never be satisfied.

Plato often conceded in his dialogues that principled living doesn't always produce the greatest worldly rewards. However, he held firm: there is something beyond the physical world, and living in alignment with higher principles of virtue brings us closer to the gods. Only when we live by clear principles does the soul achieve its deepest contentment. Plato fundamentally shifted how Greeks—and later Romans—understood human nature. It's no coincidence that soon after Plato, more complex, interdependent cities and democracies begin to emerge.

Corrupted Forms

If Plato's model feels vaguely familiar, it's because you've likely heard it before. 2,300 years later, an Austrian student named Sigmund Freud develops an obsession with Plato's dialogues.

Freud received a rigorous classical education in Austria and was fluent in both Greek and Latin. At seventeen, for his final exam, he translated a passage from Sophocles' Oedipus Rex—the play that would later inspire his most famous and controversial theory.

Freud's early patients were primarily women suffering from mysterious paralysis and seizures with no identifiable cause. Doctors branded them "hysterics" and sent them home. Freud became curious. He began sensing their symptoms weren't just physical. Psychology in the 19th century was still in its infancy, and the mind was a black box—you were either sane or insane. Mental health equaled personal control, and that was the end of the story. There was no model for understanding the mind. Vienna in the 19th century was the pinnacle of Victorian culture and saturated with repression. It makes Freud start to wonder: when we bottle up desire, where does it go? In 1923, he publishes The Ego and the Id, which introduces his model of the human mind, structured in *three parts.*

The Id: This is the chaotic, dark, and demanding reservoir of our basic instincts. It operates entirely on the "Pleasure Principle," screaming for immediate gratification without regard for logic or consequence.

The Ego: This is the "I" caught in the crossfire. The Ego's job is to balance the impossible demands of the wild Id with the harsh realities of the external world.

The Superego: This is the internalized voice of morality. It is the "Moral Principle," constantly judging us and demanding we be "perfect," often to an unrealistic and punishing degree.

When Freud sat down to map the human psyche, he didn't start from scratch. He borrows Plato's tripartite chariot and rebrands it. But that's not all he borrows. He also "invents" a therapy method built on *continuous questioning.* The method involved asking simple questions with inquisitive neutrality. The practitioner becomes a blank mirror, reflecting the client's unconscious patterns back to them. He calls it the "talking cure."

Freud: "What brings you in?"

Dora: "I've had an uncontrollable cough that is becoming unmanageable."

Freud: "When did the cough begin?"

Dora: "Two years ago, when I was sixteen."

Freud: "Tell me what was happening in your life then."

The inquisitive questioning is designed to reveal the patient's inner world. The goal is for patients to reach a "productive confusion" where they begin to recognize their unconscious patterns. Sound familiar?

He never openly admits it, but the similarities between Freud's Psychoanalysis and the Socratic Method are too obvious to ignore. Are we supposed to believe that Freud, who obsessively studies Greek philosophy, suddenly "invents" something that directly mirrors Plato and Socrates in both model and process? Study Plato and Socrates closely enough, and you can't unsee it—Freud rips them off.

The West's most celebrated psychologist hoists his reputation on the shoulders of the Greeks. As unflattering as that may be for Freud, that's not what I find interesting about this story. In 1927, Philosopher Alfred North Whitehead said, "The entire history of Western thought is a series of footnotes to Plato." There are over 500,000 licensed therapists in the US today who have delivered around 20 billion therapy sessions, the vast majority of which use Freud's Psychoanalysis. I didn't really understand what Whitehead meant until I made this connection. Plato's Chariot and the Socratic Method are very much alive today, perhaps more alive than ever. They saturate our lives. They shape how we think about our minds and how we heal them. Every time we reference our "ego," we reference Plato's Chariot. Every time we go to therapy, we're practicing the Socratic Method rebranded. What I find more interesting is the *differences* between Freud and the Greeks.

Freud's controversies are well documented, including his cocaine use and his tendency to fall in love with patients. However, few people know the true origin of his most influential theory and the depth of his corruption. The Oedipus Theory, proposed originally in 1899, states that young children unconsciously sexually desire their opposite-sex parent, a cornerstone of Western psychology. Early in his career, Freud worked with patients who experienced childhood sexual abuse during his studies in Paris. Initially, he sympathizes deeply with these stories, empathizing with their trauma. Then, suddenly, when Freud turns thirty-five, something changes. His work starts drawing attention to high-seated members of Viennese society who, Freud alleges, are raping their children. Acknowledging children's abuse stories meant accusing respected community members of rape. The Viennese couldn't stomach this and Freud becomes an outcast. He's no longer invited to parties and begins to grow a reputation as a disruptor. In 1897, he suddenly develops the Oedipus complex. Abused children? They were the ones fantasizing about it— they wanted their fathers. No, parents couldn't be blamed. Children were raped, and Freud gave Vienna a convenient answer: blame the children.

Why would Freud do something so unthinkable? The answer was buried until Jeffrey Masson, a curator of the Sigmund Freud Archives, gained full access to Freud's private letters. What he discovers in 1984 is damning: The letters reveal that Freud developed the Oedipus complex to save his reputation by making peace with the Viennese elite he had formerly accused. He knew he was lying. Freud was navigating tricky waters. He had just accused the most powerful members of society of raping their own children. When Masson attempted to publish these findings, he was permanently banned from the Freud Archives. But he had copied the letters. The evidence was overwhelming: Freud witnessed child abuse and shifted the blame to the children to save his reputation.

If Plato were alive today, he'd likely use Freud as a case study on the dangers of bypassing ethics and the destructive power of intelligence in the absence of moral principle. It's what happens when we prioritize our identity, the well-tamed horse, over principles. Freud borrows Plato's map of the soul and Socrates' method of healing it, but he neglects the most essential element: a commitment to truth and virtue. This isn't semantics, it's the whole point.

Freud, when faced with a choice between truth and reputation, chooses reputation. His 'Tamed Horse' wins over higher principles. He betrays the integrity of the sacred methods he borrows. But worse than that, he betrays his patients. He betrays abused children.

For all his genius, Freud ignores the most important aspect of the Socratic Method: *the person facilitating it*. What makes Socrates unique isn't his theories (he had none), but his devotion to his students' spiritual development. Socrates was surrounded by wealthy hedonists and could have easily succumbed to a life of pleasure. He instead chose a life of purpose. He knew that healing doesn't happen merely from reflecting the unconscious, as Freud did—that's only the first step. *Aporia*. Healing happens by replacing bad principles with better ones, so their lives become more aligned with virtue. This is what genuinely improved lives. He knew that for anyone to go through this vulnerable process, he must embody those virtues himself. Embody virtue before sharing virtue. He won hearts in a way that can only be won through immaculate integrity. More important than his ideas were the way he demonstrated them, sitting with prostitutes and kings alike; his courageous acts sent ripples through the history of human consciousness. He wasn't teaching theory. He demonstrated a principled way of living that others could follow. Without his character, his ideas are worthless. We often weigh historical figures by their ideas and ignore the importance of their living example. If an idea travels through a person with unscrupulous morals, it's difficult to trust it. Why should we follow them? This is always the question that must be answered before taking in new information. It's easy to intellectualize ideas and forget that what's more important is the trusted connections that create the grounds for them to be transferred. Ideas endure only when they travel through trustworthy people. Socrates' method endures because of *who he is*.

Dr. Laurence Heller, creator of the NARM therapy method, once told me, "What therapists actually do at the deepest level is lend their inner process to their clients for 60 minutes." You can't lend someone something you don't have. Freud lacks the principled way of life and the spiritual connection of Socrates and Plato, so what he's actually giving the world is corrupt and devoid of wisdom. A head without a heart; a body without a soul. What Socrates really teaches us is a way of living that brings miraculous transformations of the spirit. History remembers him as a great logical thinker, and he was that. But in truth, he was closer to a mystic.

The flaw of Psychoanalysis is that it focuses on documenting problems rather than making them better. Freud makes no attempt to help patients examine their principles and inspire in them to the virtuous ethical standards of the Greeks. He couldn't, because he didn't live that way himself. If actions express priorities, as Gandhi stated, Freud's priority was his reputation, a stark contrast to Plato and Socrates, who lived with immaculate discipline. Their work wasn't just intellectual; it was the pursuit of a higher way of living, using intellect as an instrument. That distinction is critical.

This is why Socrates and Plato's work is more important than ever. Not because of their ideas, but because of the way they lived. If history is any evidence, no idea will ever sway us all into spontaneous connection. Our shared values once came from religion, a shared belief in recreating a life on earth that emulates a higher realm. It gave us shared purpose and something to strive for together. In a world that no longer trusts religion, where do we find shared purpose? If we can't agree on what it means to live a virtuous life, how could we ever create a virtuous world? This is why Plato and Socrates' work is still so important. They knew that a sound society must rest on clear principles that we demand our leaders live by. Ideas are dead. It's why both Socrates and other ancient mystics never wrote anything down. When we don't write ideas down, we can't use them to bypass the work of embodying them. They must be shared through example.

The next chapter of the story is devastating. Freud becomes a celebrity, and his model monopolizes the Western psyche for a century. Freud's methods are still taught in psychology programs today. I learn them in high school in a 9th-grade Intro to Psychology course. Millions of mental health professionals are trained on this foundation, carrying the imprint of his moral corruption. Entire generations learned to doubt patients' abuse, to interpret trauma as sexual fantasy, and to pathologize victims.

The Socratic Method is the best process we've ever discovered for healing the unconscious mind. But severed from Socrates' commitment to virtuous living, it became history's most sophisticated instrument of manipulation.

Revising Plato

Plato and Socrates were geniuses. Reading the dialogues has made me a better person. Every time I return to them, I rediscover a beautiful, lost way of life and a vision of what our world might someday become.

But I can also feel something missing—a blind spot I couldn't name, though I sensed it every time I read them. Principles are important, but they are only half the battle. Just as the best musicians have a mysterious spiritual connection, the soul also needs a connection to something beyond the material world. Something that doesn't come from our rational minds. And while it might sound bold to question one of the greatest minds in history, not even Plato is above challenge.

Socrates, I'm certain, would be delighted.

78

Part Two:

The Limits of Logic

Making Music: Spirit

Yes, principles are essential to making beautiful music. But it's not the full picture.

The best musicians also have a mysterious spiritual connection that is uniquely theirs.

The soul needs a connection to something beyond the material world.

Le Corbusier

It's Paris, 1928. A group of wealthy socialites gathers for an evening of wine and conversation in a townhouse in the 16th arrondissement. Crystal chandeliers cast warm light over the carefully arranged velvet furniture.

The host starts to hear nervous whispers. A man she doesn't recognize is behaving strangely, muttering under his breath. Tape measure in hand, he's measuring the distance between the chaise lounge and the window. "This is all wrong," he says. "Your sofa blocks optimal sightlines. The chandelier hangs fourteen centimeters too low." He recruits two guests to help him rearrange the furniture. The hostess watches, stunned by this man's social obliviousness. She never invites him back.

The man's name is Charles-Édouard Jeanneret, later known as Le Corbusier (the Raven-like one). He wore perfectly round glasses and spoke with the precision of a mathematician. He woke up every morning at the same time, did the same calisthenics routine, and wore a neatly tailored black suit with black bowtie. His face was a landscape of deep ridges and weathered skin, pulled taut over a prominent, furrowed brow. There's a sharp geometry to his nose and thin mouth.

Growing up, Le Corbusier was not like other boys. He was born in 1887 in the Swiss town of La Chaux-de-Fonds to a father who was a watchmaker and a mother who taught classical piano. He organized his toys according to a taxonomy he invented —sorting them first by material composition, then by geometric principle. At age nine, he drew his bedroom to scale on graph paper and asked his parents to rearrange the furniture for "optimal circulation." Autism wouldn't be diagnosed for another half-century, so we can't say for sure whether Le Corbusier was Autistic, but all the signs are there. Despite his tendencies, Le Corbusier would soon become one of the most influential architects and city planners in history, designing over 300 buildings worldwide. His precision was legendary. A friend who visited his studio once remarked that it was "clean enough to perform surgery." He once allegedly fired an assistant for moving a pencil from its assigned position. In his influential book "Towards a New Architecture", he praises "the Platonic architecture" of the Greeks, Egyptians, and Romans and talks about "primary forms" derived from geometry. "Human habitation should be no different from an engineering problem—calculate the minimum space required for each function, eliminate unnecessary ornamentation, and create perfect use of space." Today, his "Five Points of Architecture" remain the cornerstone of architecture education. His vision altered the DNA of the modern city, transforming the way planners think about urban space. History would prove Le Corbusier epically, catastrophically *wrong*.

Thousands of miles away, in the tropical wilderness of central Brazil, a group of city planners was about to put Le Corbusier's ideas to their ultimate test. Recently elected president Juscelino Kubitschek had a vision: Brazil needed a new capital to symbolize its march toward modernization. Old coastal towns were too closely tied to the colonial past, so a new city would be built from scratch, designed using the most advanced technology and urban planning. A city of the future. To design it, he chooses Lucio Costa, a young, up-and-coming city planner, to lead the project. Costa designs the city like an airplane when viewed from above. The government buildings would occupy the "cockpit," residential areas would fill the "wings," and massive highways would connect everything in perfect geometric harmony. Costa calculated optimal distances between buildings, planned sight lines to create maximum visual harmony, and designed green spaces using strict formulas. Nothing was left to chance. His city was to be a living laboratory of perfect human cohabitation. Costa was a Le Corbusier *devotee*.

The construction of Brasília was breathtaking in its scope and speed. In just four years, an entire city rose from the empty savanna. The government buildings were magnificent—soaring concrete curves that seemed to defy gravity. The residential blocks were perfect superquadras, each with an optimized mix of apartments, schools, and commercial spaces. Costa believed they had solved the human habitation puzzle. They had Le Corbusier's principles. They had the backing of a president and the admiration of the architectural world. What could go wrong?

The first signs of trouble appeared weeks after opening. Journalists visiting the new capital reported an eerie emptiness. "Walking through Brasília," wrote American Journalist Robert Harvey in 1961, "feels like touring a beautiful mausoleum. Everything is perfectly designed, and perfectly dead." Teachers in Brasília's schools reported heightened levels of depression and anxiety. Dr. Maria Santos, a child psychologist brought in by the city, discovered that children living in Brasília consistently drew pictures of their new home as empty boxes connected by straight lines, while their drawings of their former neighborhoods were filled with people, curves, and spontaneous details. "It's as if the city trained them to think geometrically rather than humanly," she said. Alcoholism spiked to unprecedented levels. The crime rate, which was expected to plummet, exceeded that of Brazil's most troubled areas. Suicide rates were triple the national average. Brasilia cost nearly 2% of Brazil's entire GDP to build, the equivalent of $37 billion in today's money. It was a total disaster. President Kubitschek found himself unable to spend more than a few days at a time in his city. When asked why he returned so quickly to Rio de Janeiro, he reportedly said, "I created a monument to progress, but I cannot live in a monument." Costa's own wife refused to move there.

Brasília was not an isolated disaster but part of an epidemic of Le Corbusier-inspired urban development that swept the world in the mid-20th century, as city planners everywhere embraced a strict rationalist design approach. After India's partition in 1947, Prime Minister Jawaharlal Nehru invited Le Corbusier to design the new city of Chandigarh. I visited Chandigarh my first time in India, after a woman in New Delhi told me it is "India's most modern city." She wasn't wrong about modern. Chandigarh is the only Indian city I've seen laid out in a perfect grid. Every intersection is a roundabout. But walking through it feels eerie. Too much repetition. Too much empty space. It felt like someone dropped an American suburb into a place that didn't want it. In Britain, the Aylesbury Estate in South London, completed in 1977, was designed using Le Corbusier's "superblock" concept. Within a decade, Aylesbury became a symbol for social breakdown, crime, and despair. Tony Blair would later call it "the worst estate in Europe," and it was eventually demolished at enormous cost. In the United States, urban planner Robert Moses reshaped New York City according to similar principles, destroying established neighborhoods to build highways and concrete housing projects that optimized traffic flow. Japan's Danchi public housing, Sweden's Million Programme, and Britain's New Towns movement all followed suit and produced similar results: technically efficient environments that systematically destroy the social fabric they were meant to improve. The rational design movement left a trail of wreckage across multiple continents.

Nobody has had more influence on how our cities look and feel than Le Corbusier. That brutal concrete building in your city, taking up a whole block with no windows? Cities planned around highways? You can thank Le Corbusier. What did he get so catastrophically wrong? Look at his buildings today, and you'll likely see. They look like prisons. Le Corbusier's mistake was overinvesting in rational order. His cities were designed based on what was in his head, not the realities of the humans inside them. In theory, his designs optimize the living experience. On one level, you can appreciate the precision and craft. But nobody would ever want to actually live in them.

Here's the problem: creating something entirely in your head runs the risk of ignoring the people you're creating for. Le Corbusier could have avoided all this early on by simply asking people how they felt inside his buildings. But he never did. He created entirely in the walled garden of his own mind. Le Corbusier and his devotees built machines for living. They forgot that we are not machines. He applied Platonic ideals: perfect forms and mathematical harmony. In his head, he was building a paradise. Instead, his work endures as a monument to rationality's shadow—a place where human beings feel like ghosts in their own lives. Rationality alone creates solutions that serve ideas rather than people. It produces results that are "ideal" on paper but deeply flawed in reality. His principles weren't wrong. They were just incomplete. They lacked something essential.

This mistake isn't confined to buildings. Look around, and you'll see examples of this everywhere: institutions created in the name of optimization, not the humans using them.

Rationality is important. It gives life form, it creates basic stability that genuinely makes life better. But when taken to its extreme, it's one of the most destructive forces. Why is pure rationality so destructive? Because it's only one side of the coin. The reason we have rational principles is to create the structures for life to thrive within, but if we don't fill in that structure, it's like a cup with no water in it. The principles fulfill no purpose.

If you've ever felt like you're living in your head, in a world where everything is working but something is off, you're not imagining it. You're experiencing the inevitable conclusion of a world that forgot an entire dimension of being alive.

The First American Guru: 1

1883, Boston, Massachusetts.

A group of businessmen gathers in an after-hours parlor on Washington Street. The air is saturated with cigar smoke. The men gathered are Boston's intellectual elite, most of whom made their money in steel or oil. The topic tonight is Darwin's theory of Evolution, which recently splintered this community of Christian industrialists. In steps someone new, a man exotic to their eyes, likely the first and last Indian man they would ever meet.

He has a quiet, scholarly presence. His hair is cut short, clean, and slicked back with oil. His long beard is meticulously trimmed, and he's wearing a dark, tailored suit. He's attractive and unusually well-dressed for an Indian man of his time. Had you run into him on the street, you'd likely mistake him for a banker. Nobody in the room could have imagined the revolution this man would soon ignite.

Protap Chunder Mozoomdar traveled 8,000 miles from Calcutta to Boston. Mozoomdar was born in 1840 in Hooghly, Bengal, during a tense moment in India. British rule was imposing Western, Christian values on Indians. The Sepoy Mutiny of 1857—a massive rebellion where Indian soldiers turned against their British commanders—had been brutally suppressed, leaving the Bengalis tense. Indians were either converting to Christianity or retreating further into orthodox Hinduism, polarizing a traditionally peaceful society. Mozoomdar's father was a devout Hindu who worked as an administrator for the British East India Company. As a young boy, he remembered watching his father perform Hindu rituals in the morning, throw on a suit, and negotiate trade deals in the afternoon. He studied Sanskrit and religion in college in Calcutta. One night he was reading a Bible slipped to him by a British soldier. He flips to a random page in John's Gospel in the New Testament to Jesus's words, "The Father and I are one." Suddenly, he recognizes its similarity to the Upanishadic phrase "Tat Tvam Asi"—"Thou art That." He reads on and learns that Jesus taught that the "kingdom of heaven is within," and that Paul describes "mystical union with the divine." It dawns on Mozoomdar: Christian and Hindu values weren't competing; they are different cultural expressions of the same thing. Everyone around him was fighting an unnecessary battle, and he had a solution. The realization strikes him with such force that he cries.

Mozoomdar began a systematic study comparing Hindu and Christian mystical texts. What Christians called "being born again in Christ" was what Hindus described as spiritual awakening or enlightenment. What Christian mystics described as "the ground of being" was the Vedantic concept of Brahman. Mozoomdar spent months in meditation and prayer practices drawn from both traditions. He did Christian prayers in the morning and Vedantic meditation at night. He found that each tradition illuminated new aspects of spirituality that complemented one another. Christian practice emphasized faith and service, while Hinduism emphasized recognizing God in ourselves and in our lived experience. Together, they created a more complete picture of spirituality than either offered alone. He began hatching a radical idea. What if Indian spirituality wasn't meant only for Indians?

Journal: Returning From India

2014: Santa Monica, California. 5:30 AM.

Hotchkiss Park. 15 minutes sitting silently. 45 minutes yoga asana. 30 minute prayer. When I finish, gratitude fills me for the trees around me that give me shade. I cry at how lucky I feel to be alive.

I devote my year to my spiritual practice. I don't work. I meet a new friend who also studied yoga in India. Then another. Then another. Then another.

I don't recognize myself. There's a new aliveness. Breathing feels good. I no longer control my life. Every day is an adventure. I'm vegan. I'm having incredible sex that feels like a healing experience. At times, it feels intense, but my practice grounds me. My heart is open and I work to keep it open.

My mom wonders if I'm going crazy. "Are you happy?" For the first time, I say yes.

Nothing could have prepared me for what happens next.

The First American Guru: 2

1883

Mozoomdar's decision to travel to America concerned his friends. No one had ever tried sharing Indian culture with Americans. It was risky—Hindus believed crossing the ocean meant spiritual contamination. When he arrives in Boston, he enters a nation largely suspicious of anything outside of Christianity. Instead of presenting Hindu philosophy as a rival, he frames it as a new layer of depth to Christianity.

His lectures drew large audiences throughout New England. He always opened with passages from the Bible, then gradually introduced Hindu concepts that opened new depths of meaning. In one memorable passage from "The Oriental Christ," Mozoomdar says: "When Christ declared 'I and my Father are one,' he spoke not of his exclusive divinity, but of a truth available to all souls who would pursue righteousness through devotion. In India, we have witnessed countless sages achieve what Jesus did. They do not replace Christ, they discovered what Christ discovered: that the human soul, when purified, reveals itself to be, in essence, a manifestation of the Divine."

When Jesus spoke of the "Father and I being one," he explained that Jesus was describing the same state of consciousness that Hindus call Samadhi. When Paul wrote about dying to the old self and being reborn in Christ, he was describing what Yogis call ego death. In his 1883 lecture in Boston, he presents a revolutionary idea: "Heaven is not in distant lands, it dwells completely within your own consciousness. What you call Jesus is not an unobtainable ideal, but the awareness through which you perceive this very moment."

"You and I are both creations of God and hold divinity within us. The purpose of spiritual practice is to clean the dust off our eyes so we can see our divine selves." He claimed any sincere seeker can discover what Jesus discovered and live as Jesus did. This sounded otherworldly, perhaps even heretical to his audience. To an Indian like Mozoomdar, these ideas were commonplace.

The seeds were planted.

Journal: Dig a Deep Well

August 25, 2015: Sonoma, California.

I wake up on my 25th birthday. I'm in an Ashram. 90 minutes of yoga.

The day before, I am fired from my job. I instantly lose over a million dollars in stock. I drive 8 hours here from Santa Monica to keep my sanity.

"Ashram" might make you think of dirty rooms and silence. This isn't that Ashram. This is the Sonoma Ashram in Northern California. "Luxury" is a stretch, but as far as Ashrams go, it's the Ritz-Carlton. The place is a fun mix of hippies and retired San Francisco lawyer types. The leader is a quiet, wise, Indian man in his early 60s with an unusually healthy head of hair. Babaji. The inheritor of a long line of Aghora Yogis from Varanasi. Babaji's teacher, Aghoreshwar Bhagwan Ram (1937–1992) was one of the most famous and mystical spiritual leaders in India who regularly performed Christ-like miracles.

Babaji always wears a white robe, the garb of his lineage. The Ashram members guard him like security, as students often want more of his energy than he has to give, so I'm both honored and caught off guard when he asks me to join him for his morning walk. The sun is rising as we walk through grape fields. There's mist in the hills. I feel confused and lost and lonely. I don't have the courage to admit this to him, but he knows.

"Adam, how many decisions have you made in your life?"

"Uh.. I'm not sure I understand your question. I make decisions all the time."

"No, I mean, how many decisions have you made that will never change? Your name is Adam. What else? "

I think for a few moments and come up with nothing. Suddenly, I feel exposed.

"Life doesn't truly begin until you start making decisions. Not half-decisions that might change later. Firm decisions that won't change. When you decide something with that kind of clarity, the universe rewards you."

He goes on.

"In all our actions, from work to relationships to travel, we are searching for truth. Truth is like a deep source of water buried in the earth. To reach it, you must dig a *single, deep well.* Most people never reach it because they keep digging potholes. They dig a hole, get bored, and move onto the next, over and over again. *All rewards in life come from digging a deep well.* Only those who make unshakable decisions know this secret."

Suddenly, I see Babaji's humanity in a way I'd never seen. I realize that he used to have a job and that he probably went on dates and watched TV, but long ago, he chose to leave his entire life and family and renounce all his possessions to serve others on their spiritual path. This was no small decision. I wouldn't have been there in the Ashram had he not dug this well.

While my mind loved the idea of my high-paying job, in that moment, I noticed my body felt relieved, a weight lifted from my chest. It was just a pothole.

Something in me shifts, and it never shifts back.

"I need to step into what I really want to do with my life."

"What's that?" he asks.

"I want to help people learn yoga."

The mist clears. It's sunny and suddenly warm.

The First American Guru: 3

From Boston, Mozoomdar moved through the American Free Religious Association circuit — the intellectual liberals of the day — lecturing to packed halls, and left behind a published book, *The Oriental Christ*, printed by a Boston press before he sailed home.

Mozoomdar returns to India to a hero's welcome. His journey to America inspires young Indians everywhere, including a young college student named Vivekananda, who would later become the first person to teach Yoga in America.

Born in 1863 to a wealthy Calcutta family, Vivekananda was rebellious and razor-sharp. Once, when his college philosophy professor stated the Indian cliche, "God can be directly experienced," Vivekananda asked, "Have you seen God?" The professor conceded he had not. Vivekananda asked the same question to spiritual teachers all over Calcutta. None of them could speak about God from their direct experience, that is, until he meets Ramakrishna.

Sri Ramakrishna was perhaps the most revered spiritual saint of 19th-century India. His life reads like mythology. He was a priest at the Kali temple in Dakshineswar, where, during meditation, he would enter mystical states that made his breathing imperceptible for hours. Onlookers described seeing luminous phenomena around him. Their first meeting is in November 1881 at the temple, just north of Kolkata, on the banks of the Ganges. A friend brings Vivekananda there. He is around 18, a college student, intellectually brilliant, and trained in Western logic. Young Vivekananda was part of the Brahmo Samaj, a progressive Hindu reform movement that sought to refocus Hinduism on its essence.

Ramakrishna lived in a small, sparsely furnished room in the temple. When Vivekananda arrives, Ramakrishna is sitting on a wooden cot. Ramakrishna recognizes Vivekananda the moment he sees him—he had visions of this moment. In a dramatic scene, Ramakrishna weeps. He grabs Vivekananda's hand and says, "You've come so late! How could you be so unkind as to make me wait so long?" Vivekananda is confused. Why was this priest weeping over him like a long-lost friend? He then asks Ramakrishna the question he'd been asking every religious teacher in Calcutta: "Sir, have you seen God?" Without hesitation, Ramakrishna said, "Yes, I see Him just as I see you here." The directness shook something in him. He'd never heard anyone answer that way. Vivekananda was skeptical but couldn't stop visiting Ramakrishna. It took years before he fully accepted him as his teacher.

Ramakrishna practiced what he called "spiritual experiments," systematically practicing different traditions. For years, he followed Muslim practices and experienced visions of Muhammad and Allah. Later, he undertook Christian practices, meditating on images of Jesus and Mary, eventually claiming he experienced Christ-consciousness directly. Each time, he reported reaching the same thing through different paths, what he called "the ocean into which all rivers flow." During one of their meetings, Ramakrishna touched Vivekananda's chest and asked him what he felt. "I could see the walls of the room, the people around me, even my own body—all spinning and merging into a vast ocean of light. I lost all sense of I and you, inside and out. Everything was one luminous existence."

Thirteen years after Mozoomdar spoke in Boston, Vivekananda travels to America. Vivekananda was everything Mozoomdar was not—tall and powerful, passionate and direct, with a commanding voice that filled concert halls. His orange robes and turban made him impossible to ignore, while his presence bloomed with a reservoir of spiritual wisdom. He described Yogis who could slow their heartbeats to near-death levels, and sages who lived in a permanent state of joy from birth to death. What made Vivekananda so irresistible to Americans was not just his ideas but his presence. His aura oozed with peace and clarity, a texture of aliveness they'd never witnessed. He was a monk, but he didn't have the passivity of most monks. He was infectious, sharp, and full of parables that tickled his listeners' minds. Speaking at the Chicago Parliament of Religious Council in 1893, he said, "Sisters and brothers of America, it fills my heart with joy unspeakable to rise in response to the warm and cordial welcome which you have given us. I am proud to belong to a religion that has taught the world both tolerance and universal acceptance. We accept and practice all religions as true." The hall erupted.

Vivekananda demonstrated something radical to Americans: the universality of spiritual experience. He wasn't trying to convert them and took no interest in religious debates. He cared about their daily habits. Were they happy? What were they eating? Did they feel a connection to their soul? He was an embodied teacher and partner in their spiritual evolution.

Often, Vivekananda asked his audience to sit comfortably and close their eyes. "Now," he would say, "observe your breath flowing in and out. Don't try to change it, just watch it. Notice the small gap between the in-breath and the out-breath. Rest your attention there, in that momentary stillness."

"Witness yourself, not your worries or ambitions, not even your name or identity. Just pure awareness, observing itself. This awareness is what every mystic in every tradition has called divine. The Christians call it 'Christ within.' We call it "Atman." Buddhists call it "Buddha-nature." The Sufis call it the "Beloved." But the experience is available to all."

"You see? You didn't need to convert to any religion. You didn't need to accept any doctrine. You became quiet enough to notice what was already there, the divine consciousness that animates every moment. No intermediary, and no qualification required. Just the willingness to turn your attention inward in self-study."

After Chicago, Vivekananda toured the country lecturing to packed halls, including at Harvard, before founding the first Vedanta Society in New York in 1894, planting the first permanent institution of Eastern spiritual philosophy on American soil. He also became the first person to formally teach yoga in the West, offering classes of fifty or more students and publishing *Raja Yoga* in 1895, the book that introduced Patanjali's Yoga Sutras to the English-speaking world.

In the Upanishads, an ancient Indian text, there's a parable of a little fish who keeps hearing other fish talk about the "ocean," so he swims around, asking everyone, "Hey, where's the ocean?" He gets confused because he's looking for something he's completely surrounded by. The story reveals a contradiction in the way we seek God or spiritual experiences. We seek it, ignoring the possibility that *we are it.* The point is that we're already inside it (like the fish in water), but we're blind to it because we're busy looking for something grand and special outside of what already is. God is so pervasive, so ubiquitous in all the miraculous details of life—it's all we know and impossible for us to appreciate. God is like air; we don't realize it's there until it's taken away. The very act of seeking creates the illusion of separation from that which we seek. How can we seek God if we are part of God? It's like using a flashlight to look for darkness; the tool we use to search prevents us from finding what we're looking for. It's like trying to see the color of our eyes without a mirror. It's like being a fish in the ocean, looking for the ocean.

In India, there are countless Christ-like figures throughout history, and clear agreement on how to spot them. Many are alive today. Vivekananda showed Americans that anyone can reach this state through rigorous lifestyle practices. The method was called Yoga.

What Mozoomdar seeded, and Vivekananda blossomed, has since become one of the most dramatic cultural exports in history and a major ripple in the collective experience. Over 300 million people worldwide now practice yoga, and in the decade leading up to 2020, it was among the fastest-growing wellness practices on the planet. Mindfulness now sits at the center of psychology, psychiatry, and neuroscience. It is now standard in hospitals, therapy offices, schools, and boardrooms. We are the first generation in history to grow up inside this collision, inheriting both the rational frameworks of the West and the inner-life technologies of the East.

You Can't Measure Spirit

Which world is better? A world where one person is the mediator to God? Or a world where anyone can be? A world where Jesus lived once long ago? Or a world where he is living inside you right now?

By making the statement that one person is enlightened, you simultaneously make the statement that the rest of us are not. Spirituality is not exclusive. Enlightenment and divine favor are myths. Humanity is vast and there are powerful beings everywhere. Spirituality cannot be measured because it looks different on everyone.

Truth Is Mysterious

The human mind cannot comprehend truth. If you don't believe me, try the following:

1. First, try to predict what thought will be passing through your head 60 seconds from now. Write your prediction on a piece of paper and set a timer.
2. Next, try to predict the next natural shift in your body position.

If you give this an honest try, you'll quickly come to the same conclusion as everyone who has ever done this experiment: You have no idea what you'll be thinking or what your body will be doing 60 seconds from now. If you aren't controlling your thoughts or your body, what is?

The fundamental human delusion is that "I" am living my life. For example, when someone asks what you did this morning, you say, "I went to the gym." But a more honest answer would be "A series of forces I don't understand moved me to lift weights." We all know this on some level; however, it's socially inconvenient to admit. It's much simpler to just say "I went to the gym." Sure, from one vantage point, "you" are living your life. However, from another dimension, life is unfolding in ways you can't control or predict. And if you're not directing your thoughts or your body, how can you claim credit for anything? Unpredictability is the only agreed-upon feature of the quantum realm. Something deeper and more mysterious moves life. It's fundamentally mysterious, a force the mind cannot understand. The mind is an intense filtering and sorting mechanism that filters the vast array of material in the universe into bite-sized chunks we can process. But those categories the mind creates don't actually exist. The words we use to distinguish one thing from another exist only in our minds. What we are convinced of as "true" is far from it; it's just what you receive from your individual filtering system. The only honest way to relate to life is that it is mysterious and inconceivable.

This all might create anxiety, but here's another way to look at it: reality in its raw form is like a series of waves. Riding waves is sometimes scary and uncertain, and one hell of an adventure. The only exhausting part is pretending we are in control.

How We Got Downward Dog

The word yoga comes from the Sanskrit root yuj, meaning "to yoke" or "to unite." This etymology is deliberate. Just as a yoke joins oxen, yoga represents the union of individual consciousness with God.

Archaeological seals from Harappan sites depict figures in meditative postures, suggesting that yoga was practiced in humanity's first civilization. Yet the original yoga bears little resemblance to what we practice today. The earliest Yogis weren't doing handstands; they were simple forest dwellers living in nature. The earliest known Yogis, called Rishis, lived simple lives in the forest, deeply connected to the earth's rhythms. They rose with the sun, slept at dark, and ate what the forest provided. Their purpose was to live with God. Their roadmap was simple, as Patanjali later explained, they sought to leave the illusory realm created by the mind and enter reality. When the mind is still, we stop living in projection and enter reality through our direct felt sense.

The Rishis didn't need elaborate yogic practices because their entire existence was already synchronized with the natural world. Yoga was unelaborate, and involved sitting quietly, breathing naturally, and allowing the mind to settle into nature. They observed that after roughly ninety minutes of sitting silently in nature with a vertical, relaxed posture, they would enter states of immense spiritual expansion. Free from the stimulation of urban life, consciousness naturally settles into extraordinary peace, clarity, and interconnectedness simply through silent sitting and feeling.

In 300 BCE, Patanjali writes the Yoga Sutras, and it begins reaching common people living in cities. With each new passing century, life became more disconnected from nature. Social webs grew, and life became more demanding; people found themselves caught in webs of obligation and stress. As life became removed from nature, yoga teachers had to evolve the practice to meet it. They began noticing that the urban practitioner could not sit silently for 90 minutes — their nervous systems were too frayed. This forced them to innovate, inventing new techniques: new yoga postures and breathwork. The great irony is that yoga became complex precisely because life had become complex. Each new technique was an attempt to solve a problem the previous generation never faced. Asanas (Postures) were intended to release muscular tension, allowing practitioners to sit longer.

Pranayama (Breathing) techniques were developed to soothe a jagged nervous system.

However, while our lifestyles have changed dramatically from the time of the Rishis, the basic structure of human consciousness remains. The capacity for yoga is still there, but it now requires more skill and discipline to access. Unless, of course, you live in nature. Yoga has never been one thing, and the popular suggestion that there's a single "original" form of yoga is false. It has evolved over time to address mental and emotional disturbances across cultures. There is no such thing as "true" yoga. It has spread in the world less like religion and more like music, with each generation evolving the tools to meet its culture's needs and desires. Some require physical practice to heal bodily stress; others need breathing to calm the nerves; still others find their way through devotion and faith. Yoga is a universal, individualized toolkit for spiritual deepening. It is not a religion, but a supplement to any spiritual path. It is perhaps the only system of wellbeing that includes no medicine and no external tools. It challenges us to solve our health issues directly in the body, using nothing but energy, movement, breath, and concentration.

My first teacher described yoga as like digging for a pyramid buried in the sand. The more you dig, the more vast it becomes. And while it is a pyramid with infinite depth, any level of practice offers incredible benefits. You don't have to use it to find God; you can just use it to fix your back. That's how we got downward dog.

I used to think my moods and emotions were random, like the weather. I would wake up one day feeling stressed, another day feeling stagnant, and another day feeling playful. Yoga gave me the tools to *decide how I want to feel inside*. That might sound like a bold claim, and this is precisely why yoga has persisted throughout time. It gives us agency over our inner world, like tuning an instrument. The Indian teacher Sadhguru calls this "Inner Engineering." It's the greatest gift I've ever received, and an immeasurable gift to humanity.

Yoga is as popular as it is today because it's the antidote to a culture addicted to thinking. It invites us into the felt sense of the body — what Dr. Peter Levine calls the Soma — and for most Westerners, this is an entirely new dimension of existence. Uncomfortable at first, because it doesn't follow logic or reason. The Soma plays by different rules. But here's what most people don't realize: when we start living through feeling, we discover that human beings have a remarkable ability to sense into each other. It's almost a superpower, and most of us have no idea we have it. This dimension is full of the things we long for: connection, contentment, something that can only be described as magic.

In the West, we live mostly in our heads, treating the body as a vehicle to carry our brains from one event to the next. We perceive the world through a filter of projections. Yogis consider this a sort of "ghost existence." To live in the Soma is to remove the distance between yourself and life. It's the difference between thinking about love and feeling the sensation of tenderness in your heart. It's the difference between watching your life and living it. When we awaken in the Soma, the mind naturally becomes less active. You stop "thinking" your life and start *being* your life.

Because we are so disconnected from the Soma today, we use Asana to reverse the physical tension that holds our stress. We use Breathwork to turn down the volume of a screaming nervous system. We are essentially trying to "hack" our way back to the state the Rishis enjoyed living simply in nature. We use the modern complexity of the yoga practice to combat the complexity of the world, all in hopes of reconnecting to something that never left us: feeling.

Journal: East+West

2019, Ubud, Bali:

Life feels like a movie. Two years ago I start a company to train yoga teachers. I wanted a school that partnered Indian monks with the best Western professional yoga teachers. I wanted to do this in luxurious hotels. The best of all worlds. Somewhere warm. I choose Bali. I call Rafiki, and he's down.

East + West is the name. That part isn't my idea.

2017 (2 years earlier), Palm Springs, California:

I'm meditating. 90 minutes in and bliss suddenly moves through my body. The voice comes again. The first time since Hawaii. "Start a yoga school and call it East+West.'" It was particular about the "+". Personally, I'm not a fan of the name. But I'm not one to question the voice.

2019: Ubud, Bali:

18 months in and we're one of the largest yoga schools in the world. I'm on the front page of Yoga Journal. The business and marketing skills I learned in my early 20's paid off.

Success tied to the thing I love most feels surreal. I don't take it for granted. At times, I'm in over my head. Business and yoga make difficult companions. It strains relationships. It changes me. My capacity for difficult situations grows immensely.

I can feel this is all preparing me for something, though I'm unsure of what.

Gurukol

In India, there is a word, Gurukol, that refers to a type of absorptive learning that occurs in the presence of a master. When you're in the presence of the right teacher, learning happens naturally through osmosis. It's not just an exchange of ideas but an energetic exchange, and only someone who has truly mastered a subject can transfer it properly. That part is important. In India, families choose between sending their children to a Western-style school or a Gurukola—a more traditional environment that incorporates spiritual training.

We get so heady in the West about learning. We fixate on information and pedagogical structures while ignoring the relational fabric, which is the true ground of learning. We ignore that when you are around a true master, you learn simply by being around them, watching them do their work. You learn not only the craft but how to use the craft to become a better person.

Education is the most important institution in society, and all the challenges we face in our world today are downstream effects of poor education. In a healthy society, successful people recognize the natural limits of success and focus on passing lessons on to the next generation. That isn't happening in our world. Those who succeed become addicted to success and keep building for themselves. We bypass the basic cultural responsibility of education, offloading it to colleges or technology. The problem with that is that education isn't just about information exchange. It's not just about outcomes but *who we become* as we're learning. It's about Gurukol. If our society is to remain intact, we need our leaders and educators to understand this. We need to remember that education is sacred and its true purpose is to nurture us into becoming better humans.

I pray for a future where we remember that education is sacred. A future where success becomes the signal to start teaching. Where we stop obsessing about value for corporations and start obsessing about value for future generations. Addiction to success is a strong gravity and difficult chain to break. Teaching is one of the most fulfilling acts and an antidote to success addiction. Passing on lessons fulfills the soul in ways personal accomplishment never can. It breaks the cycle.

God Is Unknown

I used to seek desperately for answers to life's deepest questions. Maybe somewhere out there was a revelation to make everything click and solve the mystery. Until I met Sikh people in Northern India. In Sikhism, they have a brilliantly simple way to conceptualize God. "The Unknown." Not "Man" or "Woman." No stories. Just... unknown.

The longer I sit with this, the more I appreciate its genius. Anything you can understand isn't God. Unknowable is God's defining quality. We get glimpses of divinity at times, which makes us momentarily believe we've cracked the code. And almost immediately, new questions arise. What created that? What lies beyond this? The horizon recedes. It always will.

Sikhs say we can never truly know God, but that he leaves signs like a trail of breadcrumbs, calling us forward for more. It's not about finding the answer, but the pursuit itself that transforms us. Each discovery deepens our capacity to hold mystery. We become wiser, more spacious, more alive.

We are not the center of the Universe. Often, the answer we need is not an answer at all, but a change in the eyes we are looking through.

God will always remain a mystery, just outside the realm of our perception. It's the most important lesson I've ever learned about God.

Blind Spots

Plato and Le Corbusier believed the path to an ideal life runs through rational principles and the suppression of our "lower" nature. But they were blind to the felt-sense dimension the yogis had mapped. This wasn't their fault — they grew up in a culture with no tradition of exploring inner life the way India had. From Plato to Freud, the West developed, perhaps cosmically, as the world's great archetype of rationality.

Pure rationality turns life into a series of problems to solve. When we retreat entirely into the fortress of the mind, we disconnect from an entire dimension of reality that can't be accessed through thinking—we must feel it. Discernment, precision, and principles are all essential to a good life. But this is just a fraction of us. The felt sense dimension is the thread that connects us to reality. While the Greeks were busy categorizing the soul, the Yogis were living in it. They understood that the inner world is not merely an untamed system of appetites to suppress, but a beautiful instrument that can be tuned to nature's rhythms.

The nervous system, when properly tuned, becomes a magnificent gateway to spiritual connection. We are a part of nature and something larger than the mind can see. Through yoga, we can feel that directly in our bodies. We can tune our inner worlds to frequencies of joy, connection, and true love. This is India's gift to the world. Our bodies are a complex symphony of subtle energy felt through the nervous system. To ignore the felt sense is to deny the very purpose of having a body. It's not a hindrance but a superpower, and we must not dismiss those who live in this dimension — they are healers and connectors and nurturers.

But those who live only in the Soma also have a critical blind spot: the power of well-utilized cognition. The intellect enables us to plan, discern, and create. You may at times fantasize about the life of Eckhart Tolle, spending every day in the park feeding birds. But on some level, I sense you know this also is not the highest expression of your life. Without a driver, the horses have no destination.

Yoga asks us to cease the mind altogether, and this shuts off a different superpower. Why would we be given this tool if our purpose is to negate it? This is also not our full expression. When used well, the intellect directs us toward a destiny we get to choose. We must not demonize those who live in the intellectual dimension. They are protectors, and we all benefit from their protection, by being born into societies with laws and governance. Those who live entirely in the felt sense risk another type of spiritual debilitation, an inability to intentionally shape life to desired outcomes. We are not living to our full potential if we float through life unable to commit to anything. Sensitivity can easily become paralysis.

This is the deep existential battle happening all around us. We are the first generation with mass exposure to Eastern and Western philosophies. The battle between intellect and feeling, form and spirit, structure and flow. Should I think this through or trust my gut? Do I need more structure, or more freedom? Should I commit, or stay open to what emerges? We are all challenged by these questions. How you answer will change your life dramatically. History might view Plato and the Yogis as philosophical adversaries. But conflict depends on your vantage point. Are rationality and feeling contradictory? Are the people who live in these different dimensions enemies? Did God design us to be in eternal conflict? No. Our parts are not in conflict. We are here to develop and use them all. We tend to get stuck and over-rely on one of these systems, and that is our downfall. The precision of the intellect, the formation of identity, and the mysterious felt sense are all capacities we are meant to develop together. We are not meant to choose between intellect and Soma; we are meant to integrate them.

Harmony is possible. But to find the key that unlocks it, we must travel back even further, before the Greeks and Patanjali, to a still more ancient culture.

124

Part Three:

Balance

Balance

We use the word "balance" all the time. But if you stop for a moment, you might realize we have no idea what it means. There's a difference between balance – the word – and balance the reality. When you hear the word 'balance,' you likely picture a weighing scale. But a scale is one-dimensional, and has two actions:

1. You add weight.

2. You remove weight.

And that's where the story ends. Our concept of balance is elementary at best. In reality, temperatures in the known universe range from 459°F to 100,000,0000,000°F, and your blood keeps within a 5-degree window for you to stay alive. Your pH requires an even narrower range—between 7.35 and 7.45. Your oxygen saturation must remain above 95%. Your hormones—all 52 of them— remain in balance while constantly adjusting to one another.

Every organ and every cell in your body performs the miracle of balance simultaneously. Balance is not something we can rationalize or compute. AI is nowhere near capable of understanding it, much less creating it from scratch. The truth of balance is that it's a miracle. There's no other way to skin it.

How do we understand something so complex and so fundamental to our well-being? Before you finish this book, you'll be able to answer that question.

The Icon of American Medicine

You've probably seen this symbol before. Have you ever wondered where it comes from?

In 1902, US Army Captain Frederick Reynolds was hired to design a logo for the Army Medical Department. He thought he was using the Rod of Asclepius (the Greek god of healing), but he was mistaken. It's the Caduceus of Hermes (a symbol of commerce). The symbol spread through American medical institutions, and by the 1950s, when historians realized the error, it was so entrenched that revising it was impossible. Today, ironically, every American healthcare building bears the mark of commerce.

But this symbol didn't originate in Greece. Its origins are much older, remnants from a lost civilization on the border of northern India and Pakistan. In the West, we know it as the Indus Valley Civilization – one of the first human civilizations. In India, it's known as the Vedic Civilization.

The "Knowledge of Life"

Five thousand years ago, Vedic civilization covered an area in Northern India and Pakistan about the size of Texas. By many accounts, it was the first advanced civilization. Archaeological evidence suggests they had public baths, sophisticated food storage systems, and urban planning that wouldn't be seen again until the Industrial Revolution. In a world surrounded by war, Vedic civilization was remarkably peaceful. It's largely lost to Western historians because they wrote nothing down. The culture lives on in oral tradition, and you must seek it out in remote parts of India to access.

The story goes that a plague became so widespread that Vedic leaders gathered in desperation. Led by a healer, Bharadwaja, they climb Mount Kailash in the Himalayas to ask the gods for help. The god Indra transmits the complete science of Ayurveda, or "knowledge of life"—sixty thousand verses covering every aspect of the cosmos, health, and consciousness. It happens through transmission—Indra pours the understanding directly into Bharadwaja's mind, and he receives it in a single instant.

What he receives is the inner workings of the universe. An entirely new dimension of knowledge that treats the body and the universe as a connected unit. Bharadwaja returns with this knowledge and teaches it to six disciples, each focusing on a different aspect of Ayurveda. Ayurveda sees individual health as mirroring the universe's most fundamental patterns. It suggests we should adopt different health habits based on the climate, current season, and our individual constitution. This knowledge was eventually codified in classical Ayurvedic texts like the Charaka Samhita and Sushruta Samhita, manuscripts that still guide Ayurvedic practice today.

Ayurveda is the oldest continuously practiced system of medicine on earth, but it's not medicine as we think of it. It's difficult for Westerners to comprehend because there's no equivalent. While it does include herbal remedies and treat specific diseases, that misses the heart of it. Ayurveda is a unified understanding of how the universe works at the subatomic level, and how to live optimally within it. Think Einstein's theories of physics, coupled with a practical manual for optimal living, a cosmology that also tells you what to eat for dinner.

Truth

Plato believed that when something is true, it's true no matter how you look at it. It's true at the subatomic level, it's true on an individual level, and it's true on a universal level. If something is true, you can see it everywhere; it's obvious.

Truths are difficult to uncover, and there aren't many of them. Once found, they illuminate our minds and bring us into higher realms of thought. They are beautiful.

Plato had no awareness of Vedic culture. If he had, I suspect what I'm about to share with you would meet his high standard for truth.

Balance: The Three Gunas

Most people would agree that balance is one of the keys to a good life. But it wouldn't take Socrates long to point out that we have, at best, an elementary understanding of what balance actually means.

"What do you mean by 'balance'?" he would ask. "Can you define it?".

Our understanding of balance is two-dimensional—a weighing scale with only two levers. Ayurveda would say this is overly simplistic. Reality is not a seesaw that moves in two directions; it's a dynamic interplay of countless forces.

I first learned about the Ayurvedic model of balance in 2014, during my first trip to India. The moment the teacher finished the lecture, I felt something inside me shift. A transmission of sorts that connected new dots everywhere. Life made a little more sense. More than a decade later, it continues to unfold in new ways. It's called the Three Gunas of Nature. A full grasp of the Three Gunas is unimaginably deep, but it's often introduced through food. Why? Because we can all relate to food. We don't have to trust anyone's word; we can validate it through direct experience.

The Three Gunas of Nature

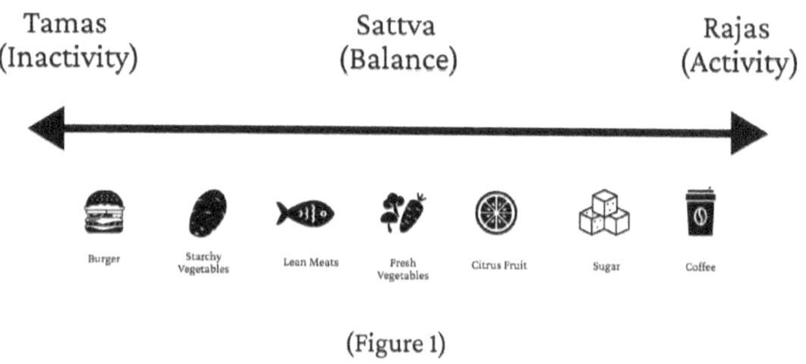

(Figure 1)

Rajas: Certain foods are inherently stimulating. Think coffee, refined sugar, or intense spices. When you eat them, you might feel energized, but in excess, you'll also feel scattered, restless, or even aggressive. Rajasic foods create stimulation and activity.

Tamas: These are foods that induce lethargy and stillness. Think heavy, oily, processed, or stale foods. Afterward, you feel more grounded, but in excess, you feel sluggish or sleepy. Tamasic foods induce stillness.

Sattva: These are foods leaving you satisfied, energetic, and clear-minded. This is the principle of harmony and life-supporting activity. When you consume Sattvik foods, you naturally feel bright and alive inside. Think fresh fruit and vegetables, lean meat, and pure fresh water, perfectly in balance, prepared with care and eaten in a peaceful environment.

The entire Ayurvedic system is about creating Sattva in your body, or the perfect balance of activity and rest. When your cells exist in a state of Sattva, health is the natural byproduct. The sense-memory of Sattva is encoded in every living being. It's not something we can compute in our mind—balance is that it's far too complex— but we can undeniably feel it. When we feel "out of balance," we only recognize it because we remember, somewhere deep down, what Sattva feels like. Recognition of Sattva is God's gift to us, a "true north" we can use to navigate life.

How do you know if you are in a Sattvik state?

- Your body feels light and in rhythm with natural cycles.
- You wake with energy and don't feel weighed down.
- Your mind feels steady rather than restless or heavy.

- You can focus without strain, and your thoughts feel constructive. You feel a natural desire to contribute positively.
- Emotions like greed or jealousy are less dominant. When they arise, you can observe them without being overwhelmed.
- Joy arises spontaneously.
- Life feels purposeful and aligned. You feel connected to something larger than yourself.

While we translate Sattva as "balance," that's not quite right. In the inconceivably vast range of possibilities within your body (temperature ranges, PH ranges, etc.), nature's infinite complexity creates an equilibrium in your cells. Sattva is more accurately translated as a "divine miracle." When we are in Sattva, health and virtuous actions are natural. Sattva is Ayurveda's essential map for creating a thriving life, a refined balance of activity and rest, expansion and contraction.

Socrates might try to poke holes in this framework, calling it imprecise or vague. And he'd be right, but it's by design. Precision has its place, but the Gunas aren't meant to give us fixed answers. We already have more than enough data: protocols telling us exactly what *should* make us healthier. Yet how often do we follow the rules and still wake up feeling off? Heavy in the body, foggy in the mind, restless despite doing "everything right"? How often do our needs shift with the day or the season?

That's where the Three Gunas come alive. It makes health directly *experiential.* You don't need to consult a book, a study, or an expert to know what's right for you in the moment. You turn inward and feel: Does this choice bring Sattva? If yes, trust it. If not, if there's dullness (tamas) or agitation (rajas), something is out of alignment. The wisdom of the Three Gunas isn't in predicting outcomes or setting rules. It's in helping us navigate the complex, ever-changing terrain of everyday decisions, decisions that logic alone can't compute. A food that's "healthy" on paper might leave you tamasic and sluggish today; a workout that usually energizes might stir rajasic restlessness when your nervous system is overactive. The wisdom of the three gunas is that it points to the body's own signal: when you feel it, you know you're moving toward health. Using Sattva as your true north gives you an inner compass that no protocol can match. It frees you from second-guessing and returns you to sovereignty. The soul doesn't need more data. It needs to be trusted to feel what would create harmony right now. In a world saturated with information, the Three Gunas are a reminder that health is something you already know in your bones. It's a refocusing on what's essential, a true gift of wisdom.

Going deeper into the Three Gunas, foods don't inherently fall into one of these three categories. The Three Gunas are a spectrum of energy (see figure 1). For example, an orange is Sattvik, but slightly more Rajasic than a sweet potato, as it creates more activity. A sweet potato is somewhere between Sattvik and tamasic, but a cheeseburger is more tamasic than a sweet potato. Your individual metabolism will vary slightly from others. What's important is not where these foods fit on a chart; it's how you individually experience them. You may find certain foods create a slightly different quality in your body. However, these are universal patterns. For example, no one has ever snorted cocaine and become more relaxed.

Food is just the tip of the iceberg. The Gunas act on all five of our senses. Go through each of the situations below and ask yourself what effect they might have on your body. Are they Rajasic (energy-stimulating), Tamasic (stillness/lethargy-inducing), or Sattvik (balanced)?

Sound: Going to an EDM concert

Sight: Watching the sun gradually set over the ocean.

Smell: The scent of lemon essential oil.

Touch: Someone tickling you.

In every moment, our environments literally "tune" our inner world through our five senses. When you go to a concert, watch a sunset, or eat a cheeseburger, each influences the felt-sense (somatic) quality of your inner world. We do this all the time: when we turn up the temperature in our home or reach for a glass of water. That's our innate intelligence seeking balance in our cells. The mechanism is hard-wired into us. Understanding the Three Gunas and how they act on our five senses makes us more sensitive to what we consume and our environments. It's a set of master keys to cultivating inner balance.

I believe the Gunas are the underlying physics that Plato was trying to describe but didn't have the vocabulary for. Rajas is the force that initiates movement and drives passion. Tamas is the force that provides stability. Sattva is the organizing intelligence of life and the essence of virtue. I was able to fully heal my anxiety after I recognized it as excessive Rajasic energy in my body. I stopped drinking coffee, stopped doing HIIT workouts, and stopped listening to intense music. Even yoga, when practiced unskillfully, can lead to imbalance if it's done without awareness of the map of the Three Gunas. I learned to create a Sattvik state in my nervous system through conscious and intuitive movement. When I became more skilled at cultivating Sattva in my body, anxiety and all other chronic inner challenges fell away naturally.

It's a Dance

This one gets deep. Stick with me.

Every culture has an origin story. Maybe they are just myths, but these myths have endured far longer than any civilization. They must have some value.

Origin stories are the foundations consciousness builds on. The psyche requires a coherent narrative of how it came to be and why we are alive. Without an origin story, we have no meaning and no answers to the most fundamental questions: What are we? What are we supposed to be doing here? The stories we tell about our beginnings create the psychological ground we stand on.

Creation myths encode themselves in a people's collective psyche and shape the manifestation of culture. Every culture has origin stories that create demonstrably different cultures. For example, the Haudenosaunee Native Americans believe the universe was created by Skywoman, who fell from heaven onto the back of a giant turtle. It's a story of cooperation between animals and humans, and the creative power of the feminine. These themes are among the defining qualities of Haudenosaunee culture, where women hold positions of authority and animals are sacred messengers. The story they told themselves about creation was one of interdependence with nature, and so interdependence with nature became the organizing principle of their civilization.

Our creation story starts with a war. In the beginning, there was perfect harmony until Lucifer (light-bearer), the most radiant and wise angel in Heaven, began to covet God's authority. "I will make myself like the Most High," he declares. This sparked the first and greatest war in existence. Archangel Michael took up arms against him. The battle shook the heavens—a conflict between divine law and anarchic freedom. Michael and his army fought with holy fire until Lucifer and his followers were cast down, falling from the sky to land upon the earth. Why does this story matter? Because origin stories frame reality. Tell your people you emerged from cooperation, you build cooperative societies. Tell your people you were cast out of paradise for disobedience, and you build hierarchies of shame.

As Socrates pointed out, stories affect us in ways we can't imagine. They embed deep, unconscious beliefs about what the universe is about. Our creation story teaches us that life is about choosing sides in a battle between good (order) and evil (rebellion). From this frame, those who value order see change as sin, while those who value freedom see structure as oppression. When existence is a battle between structure and freedom, violence is inevitable. What's hidden in the psyche tends to play out in reality. Origin stories become an unconscious driver of belief and a permission structure for behavior. The result has been centuries of conflict and warfare in the name of this central psychological projection: Order vs. change; structure vs. freedom, Heaven vs. Lucifer. Generation after generation has been trained to believe that conflict is the inevitable relationship between these forces. From crusades and inquisitions to revolutions and ideological wars, all our conflicts replay this theme as a massive psychological projection.

Why is this important? Vedic culture had a very different creation story: the Three Gunas. Reality is not a battlefield, but a dynamic dance between Rajas, Tamas, and Sattva. It's a peaceful, collaborative origin story. Creation isn't a war, it's a performance. Like partners on a stage, the three forces move together, cooperating to bring life and beauty into existence.

These forces are not at odds; actually, they *depend on each other.* Rajas brings the energy for change and creation, but without the form and stability of Tamas, that energy dissipates into nothingness. Tamas brings structure and conservation, but without Rajas to animate it, it collapses into lifeless inertia. Sattva emerges when the two find their perfect harmony, creating the conditions for consciousness, beauty, and flourishing. It's no coincidence that India has remained largely peaceful over the last few centuries, despite its religious, linguistic, and cultural diversity.

Here's the secret of the American medical symbol: It's Ayurvedic. The staff represents the spine, the central energetic axis of balance (Sattva). The two serpents represent the dance of opposing forces—Rajas and Tamas, activity and rest, the polarities that collaborate to create life. Go to remote places in North India, and you'll find it inscribed in buildings.

It may be a coincidence that an Ayurvedic symbol decorates every medical institution in America. Or, perhaps, as Einstein once said, "Coincidence is just God's way of staying anonymous."

Journal: Lockdown

March, 2020. Portland, OR

I land in Portland. First time in the US in 18 months. Airport is empty. Roads empty. Grocery stores closed.

I own nothing. I buy a house in the woods with no neighbors. I buy a Tesla. I turn 30. I'm deep in Indian spiritual practice. It's hard to connect with the world I grew up in.

Western life intimidates me. It's the source of evil. It's destroying the world. Everything around me feels wrong. I am repulsed by my people.

I retreat inward and find peace. There's heaviness in my soul. Why did I leave? Why did I come home?

I sleep on a mattress on the floor. I live with a single fork, knife and spoon. I refuse to eat meat.

I don't know it at the time, but my soul is calling me to relearn my own culture.

We Are Art

Psychology is trendy. Every generation, new trends emerge to cover the blind spots of the previous.

Psychoanalysis mapped the unconscious but didn't touch behavior. Behaviorism shifted to measurable results. Humanistic Psychology reacted to the clinical coldness of Behaviorism. Somatics reacted to body-ignorance in all of the above. Each is valuable yet incomplete.

All mental health diagnoses are based on self-reporting. Not a single mental disorder has any biological basis. There are zero biomarkers for anxiety, depression, autism, schizophrenia, or addiction. They are essentially educated guesses; we don't understand how they form or what they are. In 2015, the Open Science Collaboration attempted to replicate 100 psychology studies published in top peer-reviewed journals and found that only 36% reproduced. There's a massive reproducibility crisis sweeping through science right now that few people know about. The more you study psychology, the more you realize how subjective it is.

How to live well is literally the most subjective subject on earth. That doesn't make psychology wrong. It makes it Art.

"And" Thinking

In their 1958 book 'Organizations', James March & Herbert Simon created a new body of research around what they call "holding paradoxes." Their research showed that the defining quality of extraordinary leaders is the ability to hold opposing ideas simultaneously.

Those who embrace seemingly contradictory ideas—walking the line between confidence and humility, decisiveness and flexibility, laser-focus and openness—consistently outperform those confined to a single perspective. These people understand that we don't live in an "either/or" universe; we live in an "And" universe. Contradictory ideas can be true simultaneously. "And" people don't rush to fix the discomfort of a paradox. Instead, they hold the tension of multiple viewpoints, allowing the friction to create new, original solutions that a binary mind couldn't conceive.

To live in an And universe is to be deeply rooted in one's convictions while remaining completely open to new information. The most evolved souls are not those who live purely in the cold light of rationality, nor those who exist solely in the mysterious tides of the Soma. They are a bridge between worlds. They weave cognitive clarity, emotional wisdom, and somatic intelligence. They have learned to inhabit what I call a Well-Balanced Soul—where the head, the heart, and the body finally work together.

A Well-Balanced Soul

Someone who develops and uses the three primary levels of human intelligence: Cognition, Emotion, and Soma.

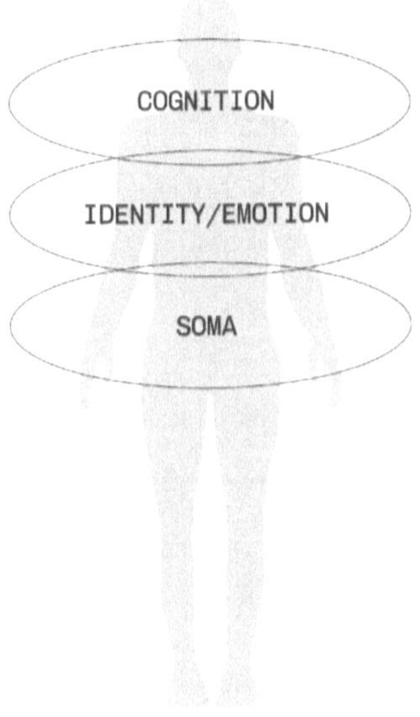

Throughout history, subjects remain subjective until we discover the right framework to understand them. The forces of the universe once seemed mysterious—the movements of planets, the fall of objects, the motion of tides. Then Newton discovered the right framework, and suddenly, things became more objective. The universe was following laws we hadn't seen yet. Disease was thought to be caused by evil spirits until we discovered bacteria and viruses. Chemistry was alchemy until we understood atomic structure. Mental health is at that inflection point now. We know something is wrong. We see the patterns—anxiety, depression, and addiction are all getting worse. Happiness has become an unrealistic ideal. We can't evolve because we can't point to exactly what is off, so our inner maladies remain shadowy and vague. However, the fact that we can all sense when it's "off" indicates that somewhere deep down, we know when it's "on." We're just missing the framework. Psychology is pre-Newtonian physics; lots of observation, no unifying theory.

The Well-Balanced Soul is that framework. It is a central organizing principle for mental health. It's an important revision of our story about human nature and what makes us thrive. It is not a new idea. It is the structure of mental health we already use unconsciously, programmed deep inside us. Once you see it, mental health is no longer mysterious, everything clicks into place. It's not a thousand different disorders requiring a thousand different treatments. It's a predictable pattern of imbalance that resolves when you snap out of entrained modes and restore your suppressed systems.

Why does this matter? Because the stories we tell ourselves about human nature shape how we live in the deepest imaginable ways. They are the bedrock of the collective unconscious and direct our lives below our awareness.

2,000 years ago, Plato developed an intricate model of the soul that told us the felt sense is merely an animalistic urge to suppress. This model was rebranded by Freud as Id, Ego, and Superego, which shaped an entire continent's self-identity. As a result, we equate "virtue" with order, control, and rationality. Order and behavior are essential aspects of mental health, but that's not the full picture. Meanwhile, eastern traditions developed an opposing view — that you cannot live well while trapped in the mind, and that the felt sense is where real intelligence lives. Much of Eastern culture took that to heart, equating virtue entirely with embodiment and intuition. Both traditions found something important but heavily distorted the full picture of what is naturally possible for humans.

Well-Balanced Souls nurture all three of their primary systems of intelligence. They are rare. They move through the world with a unique, integrated power:

Cognitive Clarity: They use cognition as a sharp, intentional tool, guided by clear principles and steady internal governance. They have clear ideas and effective communication, and the intentionality to follow through.

Emotional Authenticity: They have a healthy, flexible identity, consciously choosing the characteristics they wish to embody. Their emotional expressions are truthful and authentic, allowing for deep, meaningful relationships.

Somatic Connection: They are intimately attuned to the subtle energy inside themselves and others. They stay connected in the present felt sense and feel good to be around. They are guided by nature's rhythms and are naturally healthy.

You know your soul is in balance when:

1. Shifting between thinking and feeling feels natural and fluid. If you've been out of balance for a while, shifting into different modes can feel clunky, challenging, or met with resistance.

2. You naturally arrange your day with a mix of intellectual or creative activities, movement, rest, time with others, and spiritual connection.

3. You can choose when to lead with your head and when to lead with your heart. Some moments call for intuition, and some moments call for rationality. When your soul is in balance, you'll find yourself calling on both in different moments.

4. Your connections deepen because you can connect with others in different dimensions — intellectual, emotional, spiritual — without getting stuck in one.

5. You can do rigorous, demanding work without living entirely inside your mind.

6. You find yourself able to resist the temptation of addictions, as you feel naturally nourished by life.

7. You hold discipline and consistency while remaining open to flow, mystery, and spontaneity.

8. You find yourself able to relate to and have compassion for almost anyone because you can see the different types of intelligence at work in all.

9. You feel naturally content, without the inner turmoil that comes from suppressing your natural capacities or needs.

10. Your life begins to thrive in all dimensions. Nothing feels left out.

Well-Balanced souls are dynamic; they move effortlessly between the three intelligences. They understand that each has an essential purpose in our lives and society. They understand that when one system goes unused, an entire dimension of our existence diminishes. Nothing is forced, and nothing is suppressed. Mental health is an effortless byproduct because we are naturally whole. When we sense someone is truly thriving, it's because, instinctively, we sense they are in balance among their three intelligences. On the other hand, we can sense almost immediately when someone is out of balance just by being around them, because the sense is deeply programmed inside us.

HOW WE LOSE BALANCE

We all have a natural bias toward experiencing reality through our most developed system. We tend to get stuck living heavily through intellect (as Plato did), felt sense (as many yogis do), or social reputation (as Freud did).

Genetics, trauma, and our environment predispose us to favor one, and we often stay there for years, sometimes forever. Cultures reinforce this: Western societies train us toward intellect; nature-connected or indigenous traditions lean into felt sense, and those patterns get reinforced over time. However, these aren't diseases or fixed traits. They're modes we can shift out of. It's natural to lean on our strengths. But this creates an unconscious imbalance that disconnects us from our wholeness and true potential. It becomes "normal" to live as only a fraction of ourselves. Statements like "I'm a very logical person," "I'm just very emotional," or "I care too much about what people think" reveal the modes we bury ourselves in. These feel like facts about who we are, but they're an unconscious protection mechanism we use to stay in our most comfortable mode. The shift starts when you get curious about using your other innate capacities. What if, instead of thinking your way through a feeling, you simply felt it? What if, instead of intuiting that decision, you studied it rationally? These small decisions—pausing to shift orientation—define the well-balanced soul. We are not "either/or." We are "and."

The crucial moments are when we acknowledge that we are stuck in a mode and bring ourselves back into balance through conscious shifts. Notice you're too "in your head"? Shift to re-engage your body and feelings. Too focused on status? Shift towards deeper spiritual purpose. Being a bit too loose? Recommit to clear life principles. These are the moments that define your life.

Courage to break habits is the essential skill of a well-balanced soul. Why? Because balance is dynamic; it's alive, moving, and responsive, while habits create repetitive patterns that calcify over time. When we rely too heavily on one of our three systems, the others go untended. We find balance by becoming like water: it flows, adapts, nourishes without clinging, and remains clear because it never stagnates. Movement keeps things fresh and alive; moss only grows on still water.

Shifting modes can feel awkward or scary at first, like navigating fresh snow. Often, we only change when suppression builds too much pressure, when life keeps presenting the same situations, showing us the blind spot until we engage it. The current plot of our lives is always revealing disowned parts; if we see that, we can meet it willingly instead of waiting for a breakdown to force the dam open. By noticing sooner and making small adjustments, we shift on our terms. We feel full when all three dimensions are active. We feel "off" when one dominates, and the others stay suppressed. While balance takes conscious effort, it isn't additional work. It's the release that allows you to stop relying on your existing patterns. When all three systems are online, they regulate each other naturally. Your intellect protects your emotions from chaos. Your emotions keep your intellect from dominance. Your Soma keeps both grounded in reality and presence. You don't have to force anything; you just have to unleash the parts of yourself that are blocked.

The soul's true journey is developing all three forms of intelligence. When we do, we thrive naturally. Life feels disconnected only when we lose touch with one or more of our primary systems.

NEUROSCIENCE OF A WELL-BALANCED SOUL

The Well-Balanced Soul is embedded in the brain's structure. In the 1960s, neuroscientist Paul MacLean introduced the foundational organizing principle of neuroscience, Triune Brain Theory, which demonstrated that the human brain evolved in three distinct layers, each governing different aspects of our functioning. The reptilian brain (basal ganglia and brainstem) handles survival, instincts, and bodily regulation. The mammalian brain (limbic system) processes emotions, social bonds, and memory. The neocortex governs rational thought, language, and abstract reasoning.

Soma maps almost directly to the reptilian brain—your body's instinctual intelligence, survival signals, and present-moment awareness. It's your nervous system, and we share this system with all animals. Emotion maps almost directly to the limbic system—your relational intelligence, feelings, and identity formation. We share this with other mammals. Intellect maps directly to the neocortex—your rational intelligence, principles, and strategic thinking. Many mammals have a neocortex, but ours is by far the most developed.

The Well-Balanced Soul describes how your brain works when all three layers function together as an integrated whole. It should seem obvious that we are in an optimal mental state when we use our whole self, but our obsession with reductionism blinds us to what is obvious, hiding the forest in the trees. Neuroscience keeps producing exciting discoveries, but without an organizing principle to define what optimal looks like, these insights remain disconnected fragments rather than a coherent map of helpful information. Said another way, it lacks wisdom.

Mental health isn't about developing something new. It's about nurturing your soul as an integrated whole, not just your neocortex. Health is the natural state when nothing is suppressed. Suffering happens when we chronically override our core systems. The unconscious recognizes when we ignore a system and begins sending warning signals through suffering, such as anxiety or depression.

The Well-Balanced Soul is the map for human thriving we are already unconsciously using. Every person we recognize as truly great is a rare example of someone operating from all three systems. Marcus Aurelius—brilliant intellect, deep emotional wisdom, warrior's body. Maya Angelou— profound thinking, emotional authenticity, powerful presence. The Dalai Lama—philosophical clarity, compassion, embodied joy. We judge or even demonize figures who represent imbalance because we unconsciously hold balance as an ideal.

The Well-Balanced Soul doesn't require a PhD to understand. In fact, it doesn't even require you to study. Why? Because we all can feel instinctually when someone is out of balance. It's innate in our perception. It's obvious. You've probably met someone who lives entirely in their head, who ignores the magic of the felt sense. They analyze everything and feel nothing. You don't need to study this; you can sense it immediately by being around them. They feel cold and disconnected. You've also probably met the opposite: someone living entirely somatically, with little ability to use the superpower of cognition.

If a PhD is required to be an "authority" on mental health, our world will remain in spiritual poverty. We can't outsource the responsibility for balancing ourselves, even if we wanted to—balance is far too dynamic. It can only be done by learning to listen to our inner signals. No system of external authority will ever create balance. Balance is too dynamic and can only be organized by the inner force within us. Restoring balance comes from reinvigorating the seed of awareness of balance within. We must be empowered. We must end our addiction to reductionism, diagnoses, and therapy, and reinvigorate a bottom-up approach to mental health rooted in wisdom. I imagine a world where we stop diagnosing anxiety and depression altogether, instead rebuilding mental health around the principle of The Well-Balanced Soul.

IMBALANCED DEVELOPMENT

Most family systems reward certain aspects of children and punish others. Intellect-dominant families praise children for good grades and clever observations. They raise children with clear values and structure but get uncomfortable when they cry or need physical comfort. If you grow up in an intellect-dominant family, you learn: thinking is safe, feeling is dangerous.

Relational-dominant families nurture children to be well-perceived and well-liked. They raise children to value social bonds and use relationships as their primary navigation tool. If you grow up in a relational-dominant family, you learn: I need to be respected and well-liked by the tribe.

Somatic-dominant families celebrate sensitivity and often dismiss structure and clear, rational thinking. They encourage children to "feel their feelings" and trust their bodies, sometimes viewing intellectual analysis as cold or disconnected. These families tend to value spontaneity and emotional authenticity over achievement or social convention. If you grow up in a somatic-dominant family, you learn: feeling is valuable, reasoning is inhumane.

Trauma accelerates imbalance. When something terrible happens, you instinctively disconnect from whatever system is overwhelmed. A child who experiences sexual abuse often disconnects from the Soma entirely. The body becomes unsafe, so they live exclusively in their head. The child whose emotions were met with rage learns to suppress all feelings and retreat into thinking or numbness. These disconnections are intelligent survival responses. They help us adapt in challenging circumstances. The problem is that these adaptations get stuck in our nervous system. The adaptation that saved you at seven becomes your downfall at thirty-seven. Ironically, the system that saved you becomes your prison. We mistake these patterns as inherent character traits when we say things like "I'm just a thinker" or "I'm just emotional." When we limit ourselves in this way, we defend our own imbalance. We mistake our compensation patterns for our identity. We defend the patterns that limit us because they're all we know. But it's not who you are; it's who you learned to be to survive.

Society often reinforces these patterns. You get into Harvard by being cognitive-dominant, not by being balanced. Universities actively punish somatic and emotional intelligence. Professors who believe in God are perceived as less credible than those who practice reductionist science. Mental health institutions almost exclusively train therapists to practice cognitive therapies.

Cognitive therapy, the dominant model, keeps people stuck in cognitive loops—fifty sessions of talking about your childhood trauma without ever addressing the fact that your body is still holding it. The problem with talk therapy is that it's the intellect trying to solve problems that live in the body. This drives many people toward spirituality for relief. But spirituality often rejects intellect entirely. "Just be present. Just feel." "Being, not doing." We keep swinging between extremes, never landing in wholeness.

STAY IN YOUR WORK

As you read this, you may find yourself thinking of all the people in your life who are out of balance and need fixing. Don't fall into this trap.

What should we do when we meet someone who's stuck? Do not shame them or try to fix them. Imbalances are a fundamental human challenge we all navigate together, and no amount of shame or judgment is helpful. Imbalance is very normal, and nobody lives in balance all the time. However, we also need to open our eyes and stop pretending that being stuck in modes is good for us.

In healthy relationships, we see each other in both our strengths and weaknesses, supporting each other's balance and growth patiently over time. Our presence alone can be a gentle, loving reminder to someone who is stuck. We are often attracted to people who embody the opposite strength, and there's growth in polarity. We don't need to convince anyone of anything. Balance happens naturally in authentic, growth-oriented relationships. In a healthy culture, everyone is a reflection point to bounce off. Some people will be more cognitive dominant. Others will be more somatically dominant. Each plays an important role in society. We are meant to embody different types of intelligence that others are blind to and learn from one another slowly over time.

The challenge isn't seeing imbalance in others. The challenge is seeing imbalance **in yourself**. Seeing yourself clearly is hard; it's like trying to read a book pressed against your face; you're too close to see the words. This is the strange condition of being human. We can clearly see everyone else's blind spots, while remaining blind to our own. It's why we need one another.

I'm not inviting you to cast judgment on others—I insist that you don't. You must not use this as an excuse to highlight other people's flaws. This is a tool to support your relationship with yourself. Ideas that endure travel through embodied people, not those who preach about them. Balance is something that can only be shared through a living example. Balance can only be shared if you have balance. I'm inviting you to acknowledge and work on your own imbalances, patiently and with self-compassion. These are not things you can change quickly. However, simply acknowledging moments when you are out of balance goes a long way.

Imbalance, at times, is indistinguishable from malice. When someone is out of balance, they will do things that harm others—often not intentionally, but as a projection of their imbalance. They think they are fixing something when, in reality, they are compensating for an imbalance within themselves. Remember, the right experience or practice can shift anyone in a moment. It's why we need healers and why everyone is worthy of forgiveness.

This is the spiritual and psychological battle of our time. We judge others while remaining blind to our own imbalance. If you accept the most fundamental principle of psychology—that everything you perceive is filtered through your own experience—then the conflicts you see "out there" in the world are projections of what's happening inside you. Said another way, when you are imbalanced, you'll project that on others as a coping strategy. We do this to bypass our own inner work. Be very mindful of this.

The rigid, intellectual entrepreneur who enrages you? That's your disowned intellect demanding attention. The tantric yogi who triggers the hell out of you? That's your felt sense calling you back to rediscover the pleasure of being alive. I find the things and the people I'm most genuinely curious about are the breadcrumbs that signal me back to my own balance. This is good news. No, it's the best news, because it means conflict is solvable. Not by fixing problems you have no influence over, but by balancing your soul. We're locked in tribal warfare between those who worship the mind and those who worship the body, between those who trust only reason and those who trust only felt sense. We cast judgment on others to avoid addressing our obvious blind spots. Reality can be a battlefield or a dance; it's your choice. Those who trigger us most hold important lessons for us—they possess precisely what we need most. The way forward isn't to choose sides between rationality, emotion, and Soma. It's to integrate. The work is entirely in your hands. I pray for a world where balance is re-established as the first principle of a thriving world. A world where all children study balance, learning from ancient cultures and how they worked with it.

A world where children aren't just taught to think but to feel, move, and embrace mystery. Math class is followed by embodiment practice. Literature that teaches emotional intelligence. Physical education that integrates somatic awareness. I pray for a world where companies value the wholeness of humans, where leadership isn't about being the smartest person in the room but being the most integrated. I pray for a world where we see relationships for what they are: a shared journey toward the development of all parts of ourselves. Where we understand we're drawn to those who embody our blind spots, stop trying to change one another, and instead embrace polarity, accepting our role in patiently supporting each other's evolution. The cost of imbalance is a broken world. Addiction epidemics. Mass medication of children. This isn't because we don't have enough therapists or better drugs. It's because we're too busy optimizing systems that shouldn't exist. Balance is not a problem to address "out there." It can only be addressed inside.

The way forward isn't to choose sides between rationality, emotion, and Soma. It's about integrating the whole, and it can only be done in the intimacy of your mind, body, and heart. The work is entirely in your hands.

The 4 Principal Indicators of Mental Health

Each of the three systems has a universal principle of health, which, in the spirit of Socratic Method, brings greater clarity to the virtuous use of each. They are universal, meaning that they transcend culture, therapeutic modality, and individual differences. They are the guiding principles that define the optimal function of each system.

Principle 1: Cognitive Health

"The ability to choose or direct your desired behaviors, emotions, thoughts, and experiences." **Intentionality**

When we think of cognition, we often think of cognitive performance—IQ scores, processing speed, pattern recognition, and the capacity to solve complex problems. the performance-focused view of cognitive health misses something crucial. Why do we have cognition in the first place?

Cognitive health isn't about maximizing mental horsepower but about developing *intentionality*—the capacity to direct our experience and behavior. It's Plato's chariot driver. Being a good driver isn't just about processing information. It's about being intentional about how you filter information and how you communicate that to the rest of your body, so the deepest desires of your life become real outcomes. This involves recognizing when to engage analytical thinking and when to step back and let other forms of intelligence guide you. We often think of cognition only in terms of pattern recognition, information retention, and memory. However, true cognitive health is measured in intentionality

Intentionality shows up in everyday moments. It's the ability to notice when you're scrolling social media mindlessly and choose to put your phone down. It's putting down the coffee and choosing tea. It's recognizing when you're overthinking a decision that would be better made with your gut. It's having the clarity to say no to opportunities that don't align with your values.

Healthy cognition is the ability to choose your experience and direct your life towards the best possible outcomes for the whole system. Healthy cognition often requires what seems counterintuitive: learning to think less, not more. This doesn't mean becoming intellectually lazy but rather discriminating about when cognitive load serves your inner balance, versus when it becomes a form of addiction.

Cultivating intentionality also asks us to think beyond immediate self-interest. Can you make decisions that take long-term consequences into account? Can you hold multiple perspectives simultaneously? Can you use your analytical abilities to serve not just immediate personal gain but the well-being of your family and the larger community you're part of? These are all the signs of healthy cognition.

When cognition is healthy, it becomes a tool you use rather than an addiction you're trapped by. You can use your analytical mind when it's helpful and set it aside when it's not. As Yogis say, you become the master of the mind, not its slave.

Principle 2: Emotional Health

"Congruence between your inner experience and outward expression."
Authenticity

We primarily equate emotional health with emotional control—the ability to maintain pleasant, socially appropriate feelings while suppressing anything disruptive. We revere those who "keep it together" under pressure and view emotional expression as a sign of poor self-regulation. This likely originated, to some extent, from Plato's principle of the "Well-Ordered Soul," that the soul is most virtuous when reason wins out over emotion and appetite.

Emotional control alone can create chronic disconnection between what you feel internally and what you express externally. When you consistently suppress authentic emotional responses, you don't eliminate the emotions; you drive them underground, where they continue to influence your behavior in unconscious and often destructive ways. Emotions are healthy when they are honest. In a healthy emotional system, there's a natural flow between inner experience and outward expression. Emotions arise, express, and then shift naturally like weather systems.

Emotional authenticity doesn't mean expressing every feeling indiscriminately. It means developing the capacity to feel emotions fully, understand their wisdom, and express them in ways that serve truth and connection. This shows up often in simple, daily moments. It's the ability to say "I'm frustrated" when you're frustrated instead of pretending everything is fine. It's allowing yourself to feel excited about something without immediately dampening it with "realistic" thoughts. It's being able to express disappointment without making others responsible for fixing your feelings.

Your authentic expression does not come at the expense of others' feelings. When you practice authenticity, you give others permission to do the same. It can feel uncomfortable at times because it shifts relationship dynamics, but healthy relationships deepen through change and authenticity. Humans are walking lie detectors. People can sense when they are meeting the congruent you rather than a carefully curated version. Conflicts are resolved more easily because issues get addressed directly rather than building up underground.

Becoming more authentic often requires expressing emotions you've been taught to hide. If you grew up learning that anger was dangerous, authentic emotional health might mean learning to express anger cleanly. If you learned that sadness was weakness, it might mean allowing yourself to grieve openly. If you've been a reservoir of suppressed emotions for most of your life, your first attempts at authentic expression might feel extreme. The more you practice honest expression, the less you build up inside, and outbursts become less necessary.

Every emotion has a purpose, and emotional health is about learning to express the full range in a way that brings growth. Some relationships cannot handle full expression, and that's ok. Full, authentic expression might mean finding outlets for your challenging emotions, like a form of catharsis or a creative outlet. This might mean taking out your rage on a punching bag, or channeling deep sadness into a poem so that it doesn't come out on your partner or friend.

Principle 3: Somatic Health

"An expanding capacity to feel the full spectrum of emotions, energies, and environments." **Capacity**

Staying connected to the subtle sensations within the body is an essential capacity that, unfortunately, has been trained out of us from a young age.

Subtle signals in the body: energy shifts, gut urges, and cravings signal to us to make tiny changes throughout our day to better align with our biological, emotional, and spiritual needs. The body does not speak in words, but that doesn't mean it doesn't communicate. Our body speaks through subtle energy shifts that most of us ignore. When you learn to feel and translate the subtle signals in your body, better mental health is a natural byproduct because we're living more in touch with our true needs. However, our somatic system is not healthiest when we can feel the most. We're healthiest when our capacity, or ability to hold all experiences, is *expanding*. This is a subtle, yet important distinction. It is possible to become more sensitive than is helpful. Over-sensitivity can become a unique form of paralysis.

Everyone has a different capacity for feeling. Some people are extremely comfortable with heavy emotions. Other people are more sensitive. Some people are comfortable going to EDM raves. For others, simply stepping out their front door is a fear limit. Naturally, our capacities differ. The keyword here is "expanding." What's important is that we are moving in the direction of expansion and not contraction of feeling, growing your ability to experience a wide range of feelings.

Dr. Gabor Maté defines addiction as "a gradual narrowing of the things from which we can derive pleasure." If our only motion in life is to retreat into safety, life becomes small and gradually loses meaning. As we mature, we are meant to feel and hold more, not to shrink. This is arguably the definition of maturity. Therapy too often teaches patients to equate somatic health with constant safety. This is problematic because it ignores the value of risk-taking and expansion. If all we do is seek (or demand) safety, we will never grow. Risk keeps life engaging and keeps us present. Someone who's highly sensitive might expand their capacity by learning to be comfortable in moderately stimulating environments. Someone whose capacity is naturally robust might expand by developing sensitivity to subtle cues they've been missing. More sensation is not necessarily better; it's about expanding our capacity to feel and experience the full spectrum of feelings. This doesn't mean you should seek out trauma and unnecessary suffering. It means gradually building your nervous system's capacity to remain present and connected. When your somatic system is healthy, you can trust your body's signals about what you need. You can distinguish between protective caution and avoidance. You become curious about new experiences rather than automatically defaulting to familiar ones. Your capacity to experience intensity and gentleness grows simultaneously.

There's also a fourth that happens when they all come together.

Principle 4: Spiritual Health - Connection to Purpose

"The capacity to connect to purpose beyond your individual self."
Purpose.

Spirituality is not a hobby. Hobbies are optional. Spirituality is like a radio station that we can tune into. It exists whether we acknowledge it or not. We all come from mysterious origins, and we all, at times, draw from intuition we don't fully understand. A healthy spiritual system is when we are connected to purpose and serving something larger than ourselves.

Spiritual health is the capacity to receive inspiration from beyond the rational mind and channel it into the world through your actions. Ask anyone who's achieved anything amazing; their moment of inspiration always comes from something mysterious and synchronistic; the feeling of something unknown speaking to them and through them. Participating in this channeling process is what gives us a sense of purpose. Without the channel, we are disconnected from our spiritual roots. You know this state when you've touched it. You become a conduit for something that wants to emerge through you but doesn't originate from your personal will or ambition. Time dissolves. Self-consciousness disappears. It's the difference between a life spent optimizing yourself in isolation and a life spent in service to something larger. The spiritual dimension doesn't compete with practical life—it clarifies it by inviting us to look deeper into ourselves. Work becomes service. Relationships become opportunities for beauty. Daily activities become expressions of something sacred. Even suffering becomes meaningful when it serves a larger purpose.

At the Integrative Psychology Institute, we train integrative therapists to use the Well-Balanced Soul and the Principal Indicators of each system in a modality called Integrative Coherence™. IC gradually helps people reinitiate awareness and use of all three systems, helping them rebuild true, long-term mental health. It draws on both Eastern and Western traditions. Most people, by the time they seek help, have been running on a fraction of themselves — thinking their way through problems that need to be felt, or feeling their way through problems that are better considered. IC works by taking present experiences and training people to build awareness of how all our systems of intelligence work to create those experiences. Unlike conventional therapy, IC doesn't focus on symptoms and diagnoses; it helps people stop fragmenting and start functioning as whole people again. That wholeness is the point.

Balance Anchor: Your Daily Check-In

The most powerful tool for cultivating a Well-Balanced Soul is deceptively simple: a 5-minute daily ritual called the Balance Anchor. It's an active reset that trains you to sense and shift your three primary systems (cognitive, emotional, somatic) before imbalance takes root. Over time, this becomes a non-negotiable habit that keeps you from defaulting to one mode. Every morning, sit quietly for 5 minutes with a journal. Take three slow belly breaths to ground yourself, and write these three words down:

Cognitive:
Emotional:
Soma:

Next to each system, give yourself a score from 1 to 10, where 1 means totally disengaged, 10 means over-engaged or hyperactive, and 5 is balanced (optimal). For example, you might write:

Cognitive: 8

Emotional: 3

Soma: 6

Look at the scores. Which mode dominates? Which is quiet or missing? This quick snapshot gives you a functional map for your current state. Now make one micro-shift to restore balance in the system (more on this in Part Four). Close by writing one tiny intention: "Today when I notice [dominant mode], I'll pause and shift to nurture my [weaker mode] by [an action you can take]" End with: "I welcome all three. I am whole."

This is deliberate training. Within days, you'll spot patterns faster (e.g., "I'm currently locked in my mind, I need to feel more"). Over weeks, the shifts become effortless, nervous system regulation improves, and life feels more harmonious because you're no longer suppressing fundamental parts of yourself.

The Balance Anchor turns imbalance into integration. It's the practice that makes the well-balanced soul real. Doing it daily will make you a more balanced person.

Predictable Patterns of Imbalance

The brain evolved three systems for a reason. When we suppress one system, we're literally shutting down entire regions of ourselves. Suppressing one system creates compensatory overdevelopment in another. This creates a series of predictable imbalances that better explain the root cause of mental "disorders."

Once you understand the mechanism of the Well-Balanced Soul, you can reliably predict what happens when a system gets suppressed. What we currently diagnose as mental health disorders are predictable imbalance patterns.

Anxiety is a hyperactive intellect generating catastrophic futures because it has lost connection with the Soma's present-moment awareness. You're trapped in your head running disaster simulations, completely disconnected from the simple fact that right now, in this moment, you're safe and breathing. It's what the neocortex does when it's disconnected from the rest of the brain.

Depression is hypoactive (numb) emotional expression and Soma, reinforced by the rigid stories the intellect tells to make sense of the numbness. "I'm worthless. Nothing matters." These are what the neocortex does when it's cut off from feeling and aliveness. Unfortunately, we can't selectively numb. Shut down pain and you shut down joy too.

Addiction happens when we try to artificially access the somatic aliveness of the limbic and reptilian system (nervous system) that we've numbed. You can't feel anything without a hit, so of course, you keep using it. The key to healing addiction has nothing to do with the substance. It's about restoring the body's ability to feel true pleasure through connection, presence, love, and health. It's about building support systems around the addiction so we don't need to rely on the hit. This is why yoga, breathwork, weight-lifting, and authentic social connection are so healing for people with addiction. Remove the addiction without restoring the underlying system, and you've just created a sober person who still can't feel alive.

OCD, Autism, and spectrum disorders are the intellect dominating completely. You're trying to think your way to safety through perfect control because you don't trust feeling or intuition. You can't "just feel" if the door is locked; you need to check seven times because feeling isn't reliable anymore.

These, in most cases, aren't incurable genetic diseases. They're what happens when you suppress core aspects of your natural consciousness. Instead of treating them with medications, we can treat them with trauma-informed tools that re-develop connections to the disconnected systems. They are reversible, not through medication that numbs the symptoms, but through restoring the connection to the suppressed systems. This is why the current paradigm keeps failing: we treat symptoms of imbalance with more imbalance. "Disorders" are not the enemy; they are a warning system and guide. They are the unconscious's messaging system, communicating through sensation. If we learn how to listen to them, they become important messengers that guide us back to balance.

There are, however, more severe mental health conditions that fall outside the scope of this model and should be treated under the presence of a licensed professional

The Secrets of Balance

There's a system for everything now, and it's natural to want a protocol for finding balance. But balance is a living spirit, not a method, and no externally imposed structure will ever touch it. It comes from presence, from showing up to yourself, regularly, over time.

Balancing the soul means acknowledging when we're stuck in one system and making simple shifts. It can feel uncomfortable because it asks us to leave familiar grooves. Balancing means awakening systems that have long been sleeping.

Opposites Balance

It's a human tendency to focus on our strengths. For example, if you have strong arms, it's easiest to work out your arms at the gym. In psychology, we call this "self-serving bias." However, this exacerbates imbalance over time. It's much more challenging and rewarding to work out your weak body parts. This simple reframe is the roadmap for cultivating balance.

We find balance not by doing more of the same, but by *cultivating the opposite quality.* This is one of the central principles of Ayurveda. We balance hotness not by adding more heat, but by adding cold. We balance hyperactivity with grounding and stillness. We balance numbness with gentle movement and stimulation. This awareness is encoded inside you. You don't need to look outside yourself.

Back when I was a yoga teacher, I was already calm, flexible, and deeply connected to my body—and I kept doing more of the same. More yoga, more meditation, more softness. I thought I was being spiritual, but really, I was avoiding the harder work of structure and discipline. My business was chaos, my finances a mess, and I could barely make a decision or commitment. I've been on the flip side, too. In my early twenties, I was ambitious, intellectual, techy, doubling my income every year while my body disconnected and anxiety took over. Balance didn't come from more of what I was good at. It came from working on my blind spots.

If you find yourself hiding in the intellect or numbing out in the body, try not to judge that part of you. It was the part of you that kept you alive when the world felt like too much. Balancing the soul is the act of telling our survival mechanism, 'You can relax now. It is safe to come out.

There's no rush; the goal is not to be balanced in every moment — we naturally flow through each of the three systems. However, balancing your soul means ensuring that over time, no parts are left out. Like a garden that requires different care as the seasons turn, our internal systems need different types of care. If your dominant pattern is in your intellect, your path to balance lies in prioritizing movement, feeling, and emotional expression. You might take up yoga. If you live primarily through feeling, you benefit most from the clarity and structure of the intellect. You might study Plato or hire a coach. If you live primarily through relationships, you will benefit most from nurturing yourself. We often speak of our capacities as fixed traits. We might label ourselves as "not a math person," "too sensitive for this world," or "naturally uncoordinated." However, balancing the soul invites us to recognize that, while we all have certain strengths and dispositions, each capacity can be nurtured and developed over time. Your weaknesses can become strengths. Cultivating the opposite is an essential practice in building a more Well-Balanced Soul

Relative Balance: One Size Doesn't Fit All

The principle of relative balance states that there is no single "optimal" state of balance that works for everyone; balance depends on context.

There's no wrong music. There are limitless harmonies, each suitable for different contexts. Some moments call for an uplifting, exciting song. Other moments call for a deeper, sincere song. Both are beautiful at the right moment.

Every day, your balance might look different. Range is a sign of health. Every life experience holds a unique energy. Rest, activation, curiosity, vulnerability, adventure, intensity, softness, flexibility, expression, connection. These are all like musical notes we can draw from. You don't need to be balanced every day, and it's natural to fluctuate. Over time, you should feel yourself nurturing all three of your systems regularly.

Every person's formula for balance will differ based on the current demands of their life. Currently, I am an entrepreneur and college president. Naturally, my life invites me to use my intellect more than when I was a yoga teacher. If you are a new or expecting parent, life may invite you to develop more emotional capacity. These fluctuations are natural and can be very healthy.

The principle of relative balance reminds us that everyone is in unique circumstances. The tendency to define mental health in absolute terms is dangerous. Instead of trying to fit life into rigid ideas—as Le Corbusier did—we must acknowledge that balance is dynamic and will never be distilled into a formula. It's why ancient masters never wrote anything down. It's why industrial wellness often fails. It misses the individualized nature of well-being and the dynamic living spirit.

Well-Balanced Souls learn to distinguish between what looks balanced from the outside and what actually creates internal harmony. They develop their inner sensitivities rather than copying what others do. The only one who can feel your balance is you.

There is no end to self-growth. We are meant to continue evolving until the day we die. If you find yourself cycling through the same issues for months or years, you may be ignoring one of your three systems. The Well-Balanced Soul gives you a map to guide your soul's development, so your whole life is nurtured. You don't need to fix your entire life this afternoon. The soul is moved by the smallest redirections—five minutes of breath when your mind is racing, a moment of honesty when you are hiding, or a journal reflection when you're stuck.

And when you're totally lost, when you've hit bottom—pray. Sometimes, only spirit has the answer.

Don't Cast Stones

28-30 CE, Jerusalem

A crowd gathers around Jesus of Nazareth, and he sits down to teach them. As he is speaking, the teachers of religious law and the Pharisees bring a woman caught in adultery. They put her in front of the crowd and demanded that Jesus condemn her to death by stoning, as Moses's law required. The teachers are trying to trap Jesus into making a mistake.

He says nothing. He kneels and silently begins to paint the sand with his finger.

They keep demanding an answer, so he stands up again and says, "*All right, but let he who is without sin cast the first stone.*" He stoops down again and goes back to writing in the dust.

When the accusers hear this, they slip away one by one, beginning with the oldest, until only Jesus is left in the middle of the crowd with the woman. Then Jesus stands up again and says to the woman, "Where are your accusers? Didn't even one of them condemn you?"

"No, Lord," she said.

And Jesus said, "Neither do I. Go and sin no more."

We must never hold others to standards we can't meet ourselves.

Journal: Table & Chairs

March 2023, Portland, OR

I am re-reading Plato's Republic. I'm taking psychology and economics courses at Yale. I buy a couch and table and chairs.

I'm eating meat. I lift weight for the first time in 5 years. My body and mind feel stronger than ever.

Models Are Wrong

"All models are wrong, some are useful."

-George E. P. Box

The model of The Well-Balanced Soul fills crucial gaps in our understanding of mental health. I believe it will help shape a better future. However, it's just a model, and we don't live in models.

Life, unfortunately, is often much darker.

Part Four:

Navigating Darkness

Journal: You Choose

"The wound is the place where the Light enters."
-Rumi

Every good story follows the same shape: darkness rises and threatens something beloved. The conflict rises and costs the hero something precious, and through trials and hardships, they overcome the darkness and goodness wins in the end— it always wins. Watching the whole terrible, beautiful thing play out, we find ourselves reaffirmed in the belief that the world, despite everything, tilts toward goodness.

But this is not all stories. Some stories are just dark.

February 2023. Encinitas, California

It's 1 PM, peak sun. I'm walking to a coffee shop on a break from work.

My phone rings. It's my dad. For some reason I'm afraid to answer.

"Hello?"

Silence. My mom is on the line too. Slow breathing. Cracking voices.

"Adam, are you alone?"

Somehow, in that moment, I already know. And somehow, in that moment, my soul untethers from my body like a breeze swirling upward. I swear the body knows things the mind refuses, and mine chose freedom. Total weightlessness, maybe something divine, or maybe a coping mechanism. I float upward, spaceship above the clouds, outside it all, above the burdens of life, some strange mercy hidden only for the worst moments. A vast and impossible peace. I am nowhere. No weight, no time, no weather.

Then matter returns. Heaviness and wounds and my heart breaks open. I sit down on the curb and weep. The deep sobs. I'm locked in frozen silence and can't lift my head. I stand and begin walking nowhere, as indifferent to the world as the midday sun was to me.

My brother Sean was 33 when he passed away, 2 years older than me. We were about the same height and had the same color hair and eyes. Our voices were similar, and we looked alike, though his face was a bit rounder. My mom told me that when we were young, she didn't have to do much to raise me because I followed Sean everywhere. As kids, we would roller skate in our basement and play video games and one time we started an NSYNC cover band called S-Street.   In high school, we shared many of the same friends. He played guitar, and I played piano. He fell deeply in love and was in the relationship every young boy dreams of. When that relationship suddenly ended his freshman year of college, he began drinking.

Though we looked and sounded similar, Sean and I were very different. He didn't share my love for adventure, travel, or risk-taking. In 2016, I found an insurance loophole that allowed him into one of the best rehab centers in Los Angeles. I'd pick him up every weekend to show him parts of life he'd never seen. We'd go to yoga studios and Kirtans. We'd talk about philosophy and religion. Sean loved cooking and food, and we had dinners at nice restaurants with my friends. I wanted to show him that he could create the life he wanted, so I made him a simple website for a catering company. Within a week, we got a call from a fashion company in West Hollywood that invited us to cater a high-end lunch for 30 executives. He took the money and bought a car. I once convinced Guy Fieri (one of his idols) to interview him for a job.

I thought I could pave a path for him. I thought I could show him a life worth living. We had good moments. But there was always a part of him missing, a numbness in the soul that no rehab or sunshine could touch. I often felt an urge to shake him, to bring some intensity back to his spirit. Maybe that would have worked. Maybe that would have broken him out of whatever plagued him. I never had the courage to try. In 2016, he stole money, was arrested for a DUI, and disconnected entirely from the family. There are no good moments after that.

Every awful thing I had ever lived through in life always had a light on the other side. Naturally, after his death, I believed it was coming. Heartbreaks, job losses, and anxiety— no matter how painful— had some purpose and made me a better person. I kept waiting for the light to come, for the light and the lesson and the wisdom that conquers darkness. It didn't come.

How do you find wisdom in the story of someone who slowly descends, year by year, into the throes of addiction, with not even a tiny uptick or moment to celebrate? How do you find goodness in a story of someone who loses all human connection and dies alone in an empty room in a random neighborhood on the south side of Chicago? How the fuck could you look at me with a straight face and try to tell me there's some light to find in that?

The day he died, everyone in my extended family flew to my childhood home, all of us packed in a home for the week, every day, a new family member showing up unannounced, like something from the movies. Nobody could bear going to see the home where Sean died, but someone needed to pick up his stuff. My grandfather and I took it like a sacred duty. When I saw the room he lived in for the last 6 months of his life, I was relieved he died. I would wish his life on no one. He lived in something that resembled an abandoned frat house, old, mostly empty, lifeless and moldy, with sticky wood floors and two roommates he did not know. There were Doritos bags, bongs, rags with puke; every item he owned was an accessory to drinking. There were smatterings of blood on the wall— the night he died, he was coughing blood. He took a bus every night to a job at a discount sushi restaurant. When he died, he didn't have a single friend or connection in his life.

We packed his clothes and cleaned his blood off the wall. My grandpa had been in wars; he had seen worse than this and was more prepared than I. We met his roommate, a single woman in her 20's from Peru who found Sean's body. At a loss for how to help, we both gave her all the money we had on us, a woefully inadequate but deeply appreciated gift. I guess we didn't want her to lose faith in existence, too. She cried. I wanted to, but followed by Grandpa's lead and kept it in.

After a few weeks, tears and sleeplessness stopped, and life went on. I had family all around, and my girlfriend was warm and wise and supportive. I started therapy. Intellectually, I could understand that he was gone. Intellectually, I knew that death was part of life, and that there might be some good in his passing, relieving him of the torture of loneliness and a life consumed by alcohol.

My mom shared that the night he passed was the first night she had slept without anxiety since his DUI. She shared that she had a panic attack every time she got a call from an unknown number, thinking it was the police calling to tell her Sean had been arrested again.

Lying awake one night, I realized I possessed something my entire life that I'd taken for granted: a small light inside me that always alchemized suffering into something beautiful, derived from a belief in the goodness of existence. It must have been given to me by my parents because I don't remember where it came from. I only now realized it existed because the light was suddenly gone. I no longer believed the world was a place where goodness wins.

Ashland, Oregon, 2024

I'm lying on a yoga mat, eyes covered, mat-to-mat with 30 others inside a large, white circular yurt in the middle of the woods. There are five musicians playing sacred Portuguese medicine songs. Everyone is wearing white.

Apparently, God always leaves a pathway, and moments of his extended absence sometimes call for an agent of magical transformation. My agent was called 'Daime,' a sacred plant medicine from Brazil similar to Ayahuasca. It came to me by chance; someone I met on a dating app had an intuition that a suddenly open spot in the ceremony was meant for me. According to this line of Brazilian spiritual tradition, when Jesus died, he whispered the spirit of Christ into a hummingbird, who hid it in the roots of a tree that was brought to Brazil to be cultivated and served through the church of the Santo Daime to help others experience it.

Day 1 was like receiving a 4-hour massage from God.

Day 2 was a descent into hell.

On Day 3, the final day, the leader invites us to stand to honor those who've passed. In this dimension, 30 of us are standing in a room, arms lifted to the sky, singing a prayer. In another dimension entirely, I receive a message to try something new:

"Ask Sean."

Tears gather in my eyes, and it's my natural inclination to cover my face to retreat back into the safety of composure, but the medicine guides me elsewhere. I go deeper into the feeling, I stand tall, and welcome it through my body, maybe the first time in my life that I have ever truly, fully felt a feeling.

Below my tears, in the intimacy of my heart, something else is happening, a sort of fully-aware dream. I'm on my knees in desperation. I ask Sean how to process his story.

"You get to choose what you remember about me," he said. *"Those who are living get to choose how to carry those who have passed. That is the responsibility of the living. You get to tell my story. What is the story you want to tell?"*

In truth, until that moment, I couldn't remember anything positive about Sean. Ever since he began drinking, there wasn't anything good to remember. I began to peel back deeper memories. I started to recall what he was like when we were kids, his spirit and what he felt like, his bright smile and his laugh, and his quick-witted humor.

I remember us playing games and wrestling. I remember stupid phrases we'd say when we were kids that made absolutely no sense and made us pee our pants laughing. I remember the day we got a dog in middle school; he felt so bad about having to put him in a cage at night that he slept next to it. I feel how deeply he influenced me, an imprint so deep and enduring that it transcended even my own memory.

"I made mistakes, and my life doesn't need to end here, but that is now your choice."

For a moment, I come back into the room and realize I'm the only one still standing. I don't care.

There are many wells within the heart. Some fill with a good day's rain, and others are far too deep for that. Some lessons can be learned in passing moments. And some take longer to play out, sometimes years or decades, they are deeper and more intricate, they unfold over time, and leave us with something even richer.

"You can put me behind your eyes and carry me with you wherever you go, and I will experience the world through you."

Today, when I look at my family — my mom, my dad, my sister — I know that Sean's death, the hardest thing any of us has been through by far, brought us close in a way we weren't close before. There's pain and regret I don't think will ever leave, and that pain has made me tender in a way I wasn't before. There are lessons of resonance— things to move towards, and there are lessons of contrast. Sean's is a sad, dark story, and a lesson of harsh contrast. His life was short and full of pain. And that pain remains inside my family. There's something in his death my conscious mind cannot grasp, but my body can feel. His death cracked something open inside me. There was always something in my family dynamic that went unspoken, a pattern of emotional suppression. We've all agreed that we will no longer let that happen. We will air it out even when it's ugly. We will lean into each other and our connection, flaws and all. For my entire life, I had lived with a blind spot, a grain of love and relationship that was not a part of my cultural lineage. Rawness. Realness. Expression. It's subtle; I'm more sensitive to it now, and that has been one of the rare gifts that truly nourishes my soul. Some gifts are flashy and visible, but often the most valuable are imperceptibly subtle. There is happiness in doing well in life and being a good, productive member of the world. And then there's the happiness that can only come from intimacy, trudging through the mess of life with others, in raw expression and deep, unshakable love.

A love so deep that it allows you to show up in total freedom and surrender.

That is how I choose to carry Sean. A reminder, a bumper lane that pulls me back into connection when I start to feel numb. That pain of his death will always be there, and that's how I choose to hold it.

"Oh, and Adam. I really want to go try that ecstatic dance thing you do. I never got to do that."

Journal: Dropout, President

2024: Portland, OR.

I want to help people.

I think about becoming a therapist.

Why do they make it so hard? Why are there so many rules?

Something needs to change.

I call the deepest, smartest people I know.

We gather for a weekend retreat in Topanga.

We debate and refine. Socrates style.

I begin writing.

I start reading state laws. A labyrinth. I call all 50 states. I learn how to form a college. It tests every cell of me.

We call it Integrative Psychology. I choose this one. I am the first college dropout in history to be a college president.

For a moment, picture what comes to mind when I say, "psychology college." Then picture the opposite. That's much closer to how we are. Our Zoom calls feel like a family meeting where nothing is held back because there's immovable love.

Spirit moves in mysterious ways.

Civil War

Robert Kellogg was twenty when he left Connecticut to lead the 16th Regiment in the American Civil War. He was psychologically unprepared for what awaited him. After fighting in the bloody battle of Antietam, he was captured and transported to Andersonville Prison in southern Georgia. Kellogg enters a hell that would haunt him for the rest of his life. "As we entered the prison, a spectacle met our eyes that almost froze our blood with horror. Before us were bodies that had once been stalwart men, now nothing but walking skeletons, covered with filth and vermin. Our men yelled, 'Can this be hell?'" His daily rations consisted of a pint and a half of corn meal, two ounces of rancid bacon, and a pinch of salt. Within days, Kellogg was covered in lice and was unable to bathe. Dysentery and typhoid ran rampant through the overcrowded stockade. Of the 400,000 men imprisoned in similar conditions throughout the war, about a third would die.

But the horror of Andersonville didn't end with the prisoners. In 2018, researchers at the National Bureau of Economic Research published a study that suggested children of Union soldiers who had endured the brutal Confederate prison camps were twice as likely to die young. To be clear, these children didn't experience the prison camps themselves—they were born years after the camps closed and their fathers were released. Yet somehow, their father's trauma endured, as if it was written into their biology.

Initially, the researchers doubted their findings. How could this be true? They revisited their methods, isolating every possible variable, and kept returning to the same conclusion. The trauma was passed down to their children, as if *encoded in their DNA.*

Researchers all over the world read these findings and began studying other instances of collective trauma. One group studied children of Holocaust survivors and found similar patterns. Investigations into descendants of the Dutch "Hunger Winter" of 1944—when thousands starved under Nazi occupation—showed that even the grandchildren of survivors carried metabolic markers of the famine in their bodies.

A group of scientists set out to prove this unequivocally. First, they conditioned a group of mice to fear the scent of cherries by pairing it with electric shocks. They then studied their children. They found that their children exhibited the same fear response when exposed to cherry scent. So did their grandchildren. The trauma had been biologically transmitted across generations. These studies were some of the first into the phenomenon of intergenerational trauma.

Samskaras

In Ayurveda, they say everything we experience through our five senses imprints on our nervous system. When something imprints, it's certain to resurface in our experience later. They call these imprints Samskaras.

Trauma – a physical or emotional injury that overwhelms an individual's ability to cope– imprints on our nervous system. It is stored in our minds and our bodies. Those imprints remain embedded until we:

1. Realize they are there.
2. Repattern them.

Trauma is everywhere. Healing it is one of the most important things I've ever learned.

Journal: A Bad Trip

2012, Santa Monica.

I'm 22. Second day in Santa Monica. I'm renting a small room in a 1,100 sq ft apartment on Ocean Park Blvd from a single mother of two young boys. We share a kitchen. She's a baker and fills the refrigerator with vegan chocolates. "Help yourself."

I leave for a tech networking event at a new coworking space. My first day on the scene. I'm wearing a button-down. I'm speaking to an investor. Someone hands me a shot of espresso.

Suddenly, time stops. I'm standing in the room but leave my body. My mind flies away somewhere far out into black space. Then, like a lightning bolt, it rushes back into my body.

How long was I gone? What were we talking about?
It happens again. My heart starts racing. I'm scared. I panic.

I can't hold myself together long enough to string together the two sentences I need to ask for help. I know no one in the room. I know no one in the city. More panic. I call 911. I take off my button-down. I'm wearing a plain white shirt. They send an ambulance.

I can tell they think I'm crazy or maybe homeless.

"What's wrong?"
"I…. don't …. know"
They put me in the back and drive.

I pray for my mind back. *Please tell me I'll get my mind back.*

I'm in the hospital. Nobody can tell me what's wrong. My mouth is dry. For some reason, I start laughing to myself. I notice doctors and nurses chuckling. I realize I may be high. A woman named Stacey comforts me.

I'd never smoked weed before and didn't know what it felt like. As it was, my Airbnb host also baked weed chocolates. She forgot to tell me. I'd had espresso only once in my life before. The combo. Never again. Soon after, the panic attacks start. It's another three years before they stop. It's another ten years before I learn that this is trauma.

The Warm Stone

There was once a library in ancient Egypt called the Library of Alexandria. Founded in the third century BCE, the library was the largest accumulation of knowledge in history—a storehouse of mystical wisdom so large it spanned an entire city block. It held over half a million scrolls from Assyria, Greece, Persia, Egypt, and India.

Then suddenly it burned down. We don't know exactly how. Some say Julius Caesar torched it during his pursuit of Pompey. Others claim Christian missionaries destroyed it. Standing amid the library's burnt rubble, an Egyptian man discovers an old book half-buried in the ash and smuggles it home. To his surprise, he realizes the book contains instructions for finding the fountain of youth—eternal life. It describes a series of rigorous spiritual practices to prepare him for the journey. It also included a map to a hidden cove in East Africa. "Somewhere on this beach," it read, "there is a stone always **warm to the touch**. Find the warm stone, and you will obtain eternal life."

So the man leaves Egypt. He treks thousands of miles to the cove detailed in the map. When he arrives, he finds a beach covered in millions of smooth pebbles. He develops a ritual: every morning at dawn, he starts at the north end of the shore, picking up each stone and feeling for warmth. Every cold stone gets tossed back into the ocean. He does this every day for twenty-five years.

One morning, he's lost in the rhythm of his practice. He picks up a stone. Cold. Throws it. Picks up another. Cold. Throws it. Picks up another—*it's warm*—he throws it into the ocean. He never finds the warm stone again.

Having faith is hard, especially when you've picked up lots of cold stones. The pattern trains you, and if you're not careful, you'll throw away the one when it finally arrives. Faith is the choice to stay open in a world that gives you every reason to close. It's a gift you give yourself that nothing must earn, not because the world deserves your faith, but because faith is the most essential ingredient in a good life.

Leave The System

Often, the greatest barriers to mental health come from the institutions created to support it. Just ask Bessel van der Kolk.

It's not surprising that the man who would reshape our understanding of trauma grew up surrounded by it. Van der Kolk was born in The Netherlands in July 1943, three years into the Nazi occupation of the Netherlands. It's the same "Dutch Winter" intergenerational trauma researchers would later study. He grew up surrounded by Holocaust survivors. His father was imprisoned in a labor camp and, on his return, was prone to explosive rage. His mother, who was cold and emotionally unavailable, offered him little comfort. From a young age, Bessel was musically gifted and fluent in six languages. Tall and soft-spoken, he was drawn to study human nature. As a teenager, he stayed in a French monastery and seriously considered becoming a monk. Instead, he chooses medicine. He immigrated to America in 1962, studied at the University of Hawaii and the University of Chicago, and trained as a psychiatrist at Harvard Medical

School. He begins his career armed with Freud's psychoanalysis and the firm belief that talking through problems could heal almost anything. The Vietnam War shatters that belief. In the 1970s, veterans flooded psychiatric facilities with symptoms that didn't fit existing categories. These men weren't just sad or anxious—they were fundamentally altered. Minor disturbances threw them into unpredictable rages. His training told him the key to healing trauma was to talk it through. However, his patients would discuss their trauma for hours, yet their symptoms persisted. Talk therapy didn't touch it. Van der Kolk's breakthrough came when he began noticing his patients' body language. Heart rates spiked during calm conversations. Their bodies held tension. Breathing was unusually shallow. Some patients unconsciously positioned themselves near exits. They were constantly scanning the room for threats and flinching at sounds that echoed combat. He realized their bodies held information their minds couldn't articulate. This wasn't repressed memories or unconscious conflicts. Trauma, he realized, *stores in the body*.

Van der Kolk began studying the work of Pierre Janet, a 19th-century French psychiatrist whose theories got overshadowed by Freud. Janet described that trauma creates "speechless terror" that can't be integrated through talk. When overwhelmed, the mind's linguistic processing shuts down, and traumatic memory gets encoded as "somatic automatisms." Janet wrote that traumatized patients become "attached" to their trauma, caught in repetitive reenactments they cannot explain or control. The body keeps trying to complete actions that were interrupted during the original threat: the urge to run, to fight back, to push the attacker away. These incomplete defensive responses persist for decades, expressed through chronic tension, unexplained pain, and automatic protective movements. Van der Kolk begins to recognize Janet's insights in his patients. This was heresy in American psychiatry, which was dominated by Freud's descendants. But it was obvious to van der Kolk that talk therapy was not working. He began practicing psychomotor therapy, a body-focused approach developed by dancer Albert Pesso. He also started conducting the first neuroimaging studies of PTSD to prove that trauma visibly reshapes the brain. It had never occurred to his colleagues to acknowledge the body.

In the early 1990s, van der Kolk became a prominent expert witness in criminal cases involving recovered memories of childhood sexual abuse. He testified that victims of extreme trauma could suppress all memory of events, then recall them years later in therapy. One of these cases involved allegations of satanic ritual abuse. Psychologist Christopher Barden deposed van der Kolk during the trial, claiming "serious gaps in his scientific rigor." van der Kolk, fighting the psychological establishment and advocating for victims of abuse, lost much of his credibility. As a result, van der Kolk's lab at Massachusetts General Hospital was closed.

Freud is hailed in psychological history despite blaming sexually abused children. Van der Kolk does the opposite; he advocates for them. And what happens? He loses credibility. Van der Kolk continued his somatic research despite continued institutional resistance. He pioneered using EMDR and yoga for trauma treatment. In 1984, he founded the Trauma Center in Brookline—one of the first clinical research centers dedicated to treating trauma in civilian populations. The psychiatric community became increasingly hostile. His colleagues dismissed body-based therapies as "unscientific." They wanted double-blind studies and systematized treatments. Joseph LeDoux, a neuroscientist at NYU, criticized van der Kolk's methods as unreliable saying "he has a lot of interesting ideas, but the relatively weak connection to the brain detracts from his message." Others accused him of oversimplifying brain science to support his claims, of promoting treatments lacking rigorous evidence, of veering into pseudoscience. Yet van der Kolk continued to follow what was obvious to him. His patients got better when they learned simple methods for reconnecting with their bodies. In 2014, van der Kolk published 'The Body Keeps the Score,' synthesizing thirty years of research into trauma's effects on brain, mind, and body. The book became a phenomenon—spending over seven years on the New York

Times bestseller list, translated into forty-three languages, and selling millions of copies worldwide. It spoke to survivors who finally understood why talk therapy wasn't working.

As his popularity grew, van der Kolk noticed something strange. "Institutions, by and large, have not embraced the book." He continued to receive more speaking invitations from the public, but fewer from hospitals and universities. While patients devoured his work, medical schools ignored it. The establishment rejected van der Kolk because he threatened their worldview. They'd built empires on pharmaceutics and talk therapy—treatments that could be standardized, measured, and most importantly, monetized. Van der Kolk suggested that a trauma survivor could heal by doing yoga and reconnecting with their bodies, and that learning to feel their breath could accomplish what no SSRI could.

In 2018, van der Kolk was fired from the Trauma Center he founded and contentiously removed from his Harvard Medical School position. Ironically, his public popularity peaked. Despite a lack of institutional acceptance, millions of people know van der Kolk is right because they've experienced body-based healing themselves. People who spent years in talk therapy who could understand their trauma intellectually while their bodies remained locked. Then they tried yoga, or EMDR, or Somatic Experiencing, and something shifted. The nightmares stopped and the panic attacks eased.

As of 2024, around half of the country lives in an area with a shortage of mental health practitioners, according to the Kaiser Family Foundation. In the US, it takes at least 9 years of study and supervision to become a licensed therapist and 12 years to become a psychiatrist. In most states, you need a bachelor's degree, a master's degree, and 3,000 hours of supervision. Only 27% of students who begin a master's in psychology go on to complete a license. For the first time in 2023, new enrollments have dropped. Licensing boards claim this level of regulation is necessary for "patient safety." But that argument doesn't hold up to even a simple challenge. In Canada, it takes about 2 years to become a counselor, with no demonstrable difference in safety statistics and better mental health outcomes than the United States.

Institutions quickly become disconnected from the people they are meant to serve. They become so fixed on keeping the system alive that they forget that the system is here to serve us, not the other way around. There's no conspiracy here. The mess of our mental health system is what happens when cognitive-dominant people are in charge of a body-based problem. We've given the reins of our mental health to rationalists, people like Le Corbusier, who believe we are best served with perfect rules and systems. The result is exactly what happened in Brasilia: a ghost world void of all living spirit.

As a result, Therapists in the US are forced to offer the only method health insurance reliably covers, Cognitive Behavioral Therapy, instead of offering what they know works best. Therapist Alyssa Nobriga describes this like "sitting in a room watching someone suffer, with your hands tied behind your back." But thanks in large part to van der Kolk, this is slowly beginning to change.

How to live well is literally the most subjective subject on Earth, and helping others with mental health is a basic human right. Humans have done it for centuries, drawing on indigenous cultural practices like Yoga. This type of healing is often branded "unscientific" by the academic community, and that's exactly why it works. Nobody heals their trauma through science. They heal through presence, connection, and wisdom. We don't need more data or new techniques. We certainly don't need new technology. We need to simply allow a more integrated, diverse mental health system to exist. Institutions will never understand this because the simplicity of body-based healing is an existential threat to them. People aren't turning away from the therapy profession because they aren't interested in helping others. They're turning away because we've regulated mental health into oblivion.

We need to support healers doing their unique work rather than over-regulating them, because healing is deeply intuitive and best done when clinicians have the freedom and incentive to improve, not when they are controlled. We need to revive techniques that support both the body and the mind. Healing is not a technique; it's a living spirit that's transmitted through human connection. It's Gurukola, the osmosis that happens from being around healed people. We need to acknowledge the deep subjectivity and artistry of this work and support anyone who wants to deepen their skill. Regulations and professional standards are important, but we've taken it too far. Far too far.

There are millions of people out there like van der Kolk, whose soul's purpose is to help others. Yet, they are shut out of the system, not because their methods don't work, but because academics can't measure them. There are also millions of people who have trained in a cognitive-based model, whose jobs are being replaced by AI. Yes, AI will disrupt therapy. But not all therapy. It will never replace the human nervous system. We must train the next generation of therapists to nurture the nervous system. If Psychology doesn't learn this lesson, it will soon die. It has to stop trying to mimic medicine (as if medicine is worth emulating?) and embrace a simpler, wisdom-based approach to healing. Otherwise, all the good healers are going to leave. They've already begun.

Van der Kolk fought for this his entire career. He was messy, contradictory, and sometimes wrong. He lost his lab, his Harvard position, and his professional reputation. But tens of thousands of trauma survivors have found relief from his work. If there's anything to learn from him, it's that you don't need to be "in the system" to be a healer. If you feel a calling to enter this work, the road is not easy, but nothing is more rewarding. The world needs you.

Nervous System Regulation vs. Tuning

We blanket the term "nervous system regulation" on breathing exercises and cold plunges, but there's something curious about how we use the word "regulation." The definition of regulation is "a rule or directive made and maintained by an authority." I began to wonder why we use this term to describe balancing our nervous system. The word comes from the Latin "regula," meaning a rule or straight stick used for measuring. When we regulate something, we create guidelines and impose external structure meant to govern behavior. This doesn't seem to explain how we use the term. As Socrates pointed out, "distinctions matter," and at Integrative Psychology, we make an important distinction between two distinct approaches to nervous system health.

1. Regulating The Nervous System

There are agreements we make with ourselves that help keep our nervous system in balance. For example:

"I never have more than one cup of coffee a day."

"I shut my computer off by 9 PM."

"I don't go to nightclubs."

These are examples of what I believe the creator of the term "nervous system regulation" meant, literally, rulesets we impose on ourselves to keep our nervous system balanced. They are preventive in nature and crucial to nervous system health. Like bumper lanes on a bowling alley, regulations prevent us from falling into gutters. They work best when established during calm, clear-thinking moments and maintained consistently regardless of momentary impulses or circumstances. To create a healthy nervous system, one of the first steps is to establish clear self-regulation. Here is an inventory of evidence-based regulations you might integrate into your own life:

Digital Sunrise & Sunset: Turning off all screens and electronic devices at least 60 to 90 minutes before sleep to prevent blue light from suppressing melatonin and hyperactivating the mind. Avoiding screen use in the first 60 minutes of the day.

Caffeine Curfew: Limiting stimulant intake to a specific morning window or a single cup to ensure the nervous system isn't kept in a state of artificial agitation throughout the evening.

Movement Minimums: Establishing a non-negotiable daily requirement for physical activity to ensure the body has a regular outlet to discharge accumulated stress and tension.

Environment Filtering: Curating your physical surroundings by managing lighting, noise levels, and clutter to manage the imprints left on your system, and creating a balanced internal state.

Work-Life Partitioning: Setting strict start and end times for work to prevent "cognitive bleed," where the analytical mind stays in a high-performance state long after the task is finished.

Information Fasting: Limiting the consumption of news or social media to a specific, brief window.

2. Tuning: The Art of Real-Time Responsiveness

Tuning is something entirely different than regulation, and what I sense most people actually mean when they say "nervous system regulation."

Tuning is the direct engagement with the nervous system's current state, using embodied techniques to gradually shift energy in helpful directions. Unlike regulation, which provides structure, tuning is an art form and requires sensitivity to what the system needs right now. Tuning means meeting your nervous system where it's at and gradually, slowly adjusting it into balance. It's what yoga teachers are trained to do. As the Buddha once noted, "It is the string that is tied, not too tight, nor too loose, which plays beautiful music." Tuning a nervous system is a delicate art.

We can tune the nervous system in either direction— to be more active or more relaxed. Both are necessary. The art is in feeling the present state of the nervous system and tuning it in the right direction. That distinction is essential to the art of tuning.

Practice: Right now, pause and scan your body. Notice:

1. Where you feel tension.
2. Where you feel relaxed.
3. Where you feel energized.
4. Where you feel dull.

Is your nervous system more activated (heart rate up, thoughts racing, feeling restless) or more lethargic (low energy, spacious breathing, feeling calm)? If you're activated, try this: take ten breaths where your exhale is twice as long as your inhale (breathe in for 4 counts, out for 8). If you're feeling dull or disconnected, try this: take ten strong, sharp, energizing breaths through your nose while gently bouncing on your toes. Notice how your system responds to these micro-adjustments. This is nervous system tuning. This highlights why some nervous system practices help, while others can leave us even worse off. If you're high-strung and stressed, tune yourself down. If you're lethargic, use activity to wake yourself up. Cultivate the opposite.

The other key to properly tuning your nervous system is to work slowly and gradually, working with small, manageable amounts of activation rather than overwhelming the system with too much change at once. Dr. Peter Levine, the creator of Somatic Experiencing, calls this "titration." Just as scientists add chemical agents drop by drop to avoid explosive reactions, skilled practitioners learn to make tiny adjustments that allow the nervous system to integrate change gradually. Think slowly dialing a volume knob.

Regulation and tuning are two sides of the same coin and equally essential for creating a healthy nervous system. Regulation represents the cognitive approach—using our thinking mind to create structures that support nervous system health over time. Tuning represents the artful somatic approach—using our felt sense to make real-time adjustments based on what our system needs in the moment. A healthy nervous system needs both.

Pulling Weeds

There's something seductive about "releasing" trauma. One good cry, one powerful breathwork session, one cathartic surrender, and you'll be free. Catharsis certainly feels that way—like a dam breaking, emotions flooding through.

Cathartic release matters. There are techniques that create it, and they're extraordinarily helpful. Curiously, traditional yoga doesn't use them. It's likely because the original Yogis living in nature didn't need them. But modern life—screens, highways, constant stimulation—imprints unprecedented levels of stress on our nervous system. Catharsis can be a necessary release valve before you can feel anything at all. The need for Catharsis is distinctly modern.

Cathartic moments clear the space. They break the dam. But once the space is cleared, you still need to rebuild. If you chase only breakthrough moments, you bypass the work that shifts patterns at the source. Like pulling weeds: you must notice your triggers and plant new responses. Pulling weeds is slower and less visceral than a single release, but this is what truly heals trauma.

Everyone is Broken

Much of your trauma is not your fault. It's passed down through generations. It's ubiquitous, and everyone has their own version. Some are worse than others. The world can be unforgiving.

And while your trauma is not your fault, only you can heal it. If you don't heal it, no one will. Others can support you. A supportive environment does help, but that's not always available.

People with privilege (I am arguably one of them) have less obvious deficiencies. Though less visible, they are no less crippling. Don't delude yourself into thinking anyone's life is easy. Everyone is broken in their own unique way.

The Six Patterns of Trauma and How to Heal Them

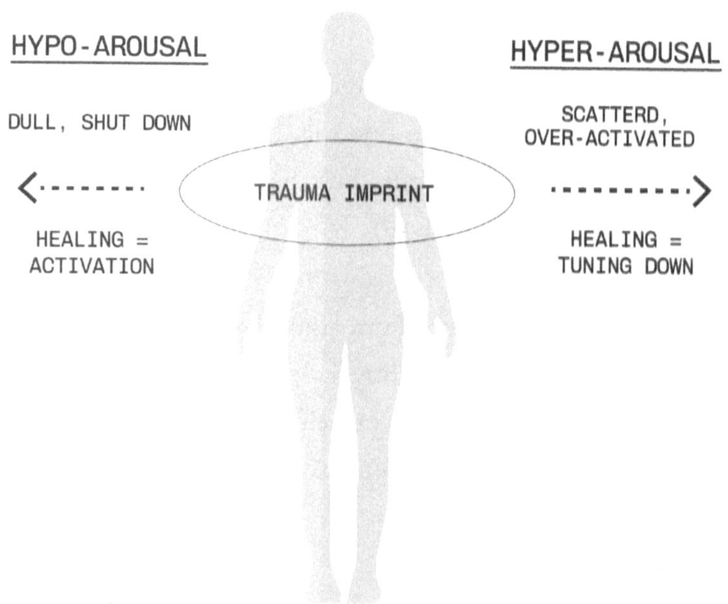

Before sharing this, I need you to hear something. If you recognize yourself in what follows, you are not broken, and your nervous system is not defective. Too often, we use new frameworks as new excuses to diagnose ourselves and others. Don't do that.

Trauma doesn't mean you're broken. We all have it. It means something happened that exceeded your capacity to process it in the moment, and your nervous system did the only thing it knew how to do: adapt. Hypervigilance, numbness, racing thoughts, and emotional shutdown—these are intelligent survival strategies that worked at the time.

Recognizing that trauma stores in the body is genuinely revolutionary, but it's not enough. We need to go deeper, because trauma doesn't affect everyone the same way. Your nervous system has its own unique way of responding to overwhelm, and understanding your pattern is the first step toward healing it.

The Pattern of Trauma

Neuroscience shows that trauma tends to push us in one of two directions:

1. Shutdown or numbness (hypoactivation)
2. Hypervigilance or hyperactivity (hyperactivation)

This is a crucial distinction because tuning a nervous system that's shut down requires an opposite approach from tuning one in hypervigilance. If your body responds to trauma with hypervigilance, practices like rapid breathing or intense stimulation will only exacerbate the imbalance. If you tend toward shutdown and numbness, silent sitting meditations might reinforce your numbness.

The key to healing trauma is understanding your unique pattern and tuning in the opposite direction. But it's slightly more nuanced than that. Trauma doesn't just push our whole system in one direction. Each of our three systems—cognition, emotion, and Soma— respond uniquely. You might have a hyperactive mind but a hypoactive emotional system. Or a hypervigilant body but a hypoactive, shut-down mind. Here's what this looks like:

COGNITIVE PATTERNS

Hyperactive Cognition: The Mind That Won't Stop

If this is you, your mind feels like a runaway train—constant analysis, endless planning, relentless worry. You can't turn it off, even when you desperately want to. You overthink everything: replaying conversations, scanning for threats, analyzing details for potential danger. Sleep becomes impossible because your brain loves working a night shift. You might notice yourself catastrophizing—taking small problems and imagining the worst possible outcome. Decision-making becomes paralyzing because you can see too many ways things are going wrong. Your mind becomes a prison, where anything unknown feels like an existential threat.

Sarah, a 34-year-old marketing executive, exemplifies this pattern. After being suddenly fired, her once-organized mind became a relentless worry machine. She couldn't stop thinking about work—replaying meetings, analyzing what she could have done differently, and planning for financial disasters. She'd lie awake at night, her mind churning through endless scenarios. Her thinking became rigid and perfectionistic. Even simple decisions felt enormous because her hyperactive mind turned them into complex problems requiring immediate solutions.

If this sounds like you, your mind isn't broken, and this is not a character trait. This is a "mode" you can shift out of. Your mind is trying to protect you the only way it knows how—by staying one step ahead of perceived danger so you're never caught off guard again. This worked once, but the emergency is over. Your mind just hasn't got the memo yet.

How to Heal: The path for hyperactive cognition involves gently redirecting your attention from your thoughts to your body and rebuilding felt sense connection. Thinking and feeling ARE mutually exclusive, meaning we cannot think and feel at the same time. To balance an overactive mind, we must engage feeling through the body. Start small. When you notice your mind spinning, place one hand on your heart and one on your belly. Feel them rise and fall with your breath. You don't need to change anything, just notice the physical sensation. Imagine sensation flooding your body. This develops "interoception," the ability to sense what's happening inside your body. Body scanning works beautifully here: slowly moving attention from the top of your head to your toes, noticing sensations without trying to fix anything. When your mind starts analyzing (and it will), gently guide it back to sensation. "What do I feel in my shoulders right now? What's the temperature of my hands?" Interoception takes a very, very long time to build. Go slow and be patient with yourself.

You don't need to be still; movement can help. A walk where you focus on the feeling of your feet touching the ground. Gentle stretching where you feel the sensation of muscles lengthening. The goal is building tolerance for non-analytical awareness—learning that you can exist without constantly thinking.

Practice: Set a timer for 5 minutes. Close your eyes and slowly scan through your body from head to toes, simply noticing any sensations: warmth, coolness, tension, ease, tingling, heaviness. When your mind starts racing, gently return attention to physical sensation. No judgment. Just a soft redirect, again and again. If there's not enough stimulation to hold your attention, add movement or slight muscle engagement to help keep your attention on your body.

Hypoactive Cognition: The Mind That Went Offline

Mental fog. Disconnection from your own intelligence. If this is you, the sharp edge of your mind has become blunted. Simple tasks that used to be easy like reading, following conversations, and making decisions, now feel sluggish and impossibly difficult. Your thoughts move like they're underwater. Information bounces off you instead of landing.

You might find yourself staring at your computer screen for hours, unable to focus. Books you once loved now feel impenetrable. Complex ideas that used to fascinate you feel overwhelming and exhausting. Your curiosity has evaporated.

After witnessing a violent crime, Mark's sharp analytical mind disappeared. A former college professor who lived for ideas, he suddenly couldn't grasp complex concepts. Following conversations became difficult—he'd lose the thread halfway through and space out. The curiosity that had defined his entire life was gone, leaving him feeling intellectually numb and disconnected from the world that had given his life meaning.

If this is you, your mind isn't broken and this is not a character trait. This is another "mode" you can shift out of. It went into a protective shutdown because thinking became associated with danger or overwhelm. This isn't laziness or stupidity. This is your nervous system trying to conserve energy to avoid further injury. It's survival mode and you can coax your mind back online, gently, one small step at a time.

How to Heal: The approach to healing hypocognition is rekindling curiosity through small wins. Your mind needs to experience success again to remember that thinking can be pleasurable and that learning can be joyful. Start absurdly simple. Maybe it's a short, fun book you can actually complete. Maybe it's a simple drawing or painting you enjoy. Maybe it's a creative project with a clear beginning and end.

The key is starting within your comfort zone and gradually building on it. You're rebuilding trust between yourself and your intellect. Every small success matters as it's proof that your mind still works.

Setting also matters enormously. Sometimes a shut-down mind just needs a new environment to wake up. Visit a museum. Wander a bookstore and see what draws you. Spend time in nature. Your cognitive system might not respond to willpower, but it will respond to inspiration.

Practice: Take yourself on an "artist's date" this weekend, something that breaks your usual pattern and sparks curiosity. Visit a museum, explore a neighborhood you've never been to, browse a bookstore without an agenda. Try a pottery class. Don't force yourself to learn or produce anything. Just notice what makes you curious and a little excited to learn. The goal is re-sparking wonder, not achievement.

A Hypoactive mind can also be a nutrition problem. Excessive sugar or carbs and insulin spikes can deeply affect your mind, making it feel foggy and lifeless.

EMOTIONAL PATTERNS

Hyperactive Emotions: When Feeling Becomes Flooding

If this is you, your feelings crash over you like tidal waves. Small disappointments trigger massive grief. Minor irritation explodes into rage. You feel everything too intensely. Emotional boundaries have dissolved; you absorb others' feelings like a sponge, unable to distinguish their pain from yours.

The volume of your heart is permanently set to maximum, and you have no idea how to turn it down.

Lisa was a nurse who worked in the ER through the pandemic. She started to find her emotional system completely overwhelmed. Minor frustrations sent her into explosive rage. She felt others' emotions so intensely that going to the grocery store became overwhelming. She'd absorb the stress, sadness, and anxiety of everyone around her. She couldn't tell where her feelings ended and others began. She cried at commercials.

If this is you, your sensitivity is not a flaw. Sensitivity is a superpower, but it must be balanced. The capacity to feel deeply and attune to others' emotional states are gifts. The problem isn't that you feel; it's that your system lost its ability to modulate intensity.

How to Heal: You need practices that engage your prefrontal cortex, the part of your brain that can create structure and boundaries around overwhelming feelings. It's not about suppressing emotions; it's about developing the capacity to feel them without drowning.

Start with something simple: naming what you're feeling out loud. "I notice anger." "I notice sadness." This engages your thinking brain and creates just enough distance between you and the emotion so it becomes manageable. Dialectical Behavior Therapy (DBT) works powerfully—it teaches specific, concrete techniques for riding out emotional storms.

Breathing practices that extend the exhale help enormously. Try 4-7-8 breathing: inhale for 4 counts, hold for 7, exhale for 8. This activates your parasympathetic nervous system, telling your body it's safe to calm down. Grounding exercises that engage your five senses pull you out of emotional overwhelm and back into the present moment.

Practice: When you notice intense emotions arising, try the STOP technique: Stop what you're doing. Take three deep breaths. Observe what you're feeling in your body and name it aloud. Proceed with awareness of what you need right now (not what the emotion is demanding).

Hypoactive Emotions: The Heart That Went Silent

Emotional numbness. Disconnection from feeling. If this

is you, you've learned to survive by shutting your emotional system down entirely. You move through life competently but disconnected from your own emotional experience. Joy, sadness, anger, and love are all muted and distant, like watching your life in a black-and-white film.

People might describe you as "even-keeled" or "stable," but inside, you feel nothing. When something happens that should move you—a death, a promotion, a betrayal—you feel... nothing. You know intellectually that you should be feeling something, but the feelings won't come.

After years of childhood neglect, David, a 43-year-old entrepreneur, learned that feeling was dangerous. As an adult, he functioned perfectly—successful career, stable relationships—

but he was emotionally dead inside. When his father died, he felt nothing. When he got promoted, nothing. He couldn't access joy or sadness or anger or love. His emotional system had gone offline decades ago as a protective mechanism and never came back online. If this is you, you're not cold. This is not just a part of who you are. It's a "mode" your nervous system is stuck in, and you can shift it. At some point, feeling became so dangerous that your system made an impossible choice: better to feel nothing than to risk that pain again. That choice saved you. But you don't need that protection anymore. It's ok to feel.

How to Heal: Awakening a frozen emotional system requires bypassing the cognitive defenses that keep feelings locked away. Talk therapy often isn't enough because emotions need to be felt, not just understood.

Embodied expressions work powerfully here. Put on music and let your body move however it wants—not dancing to perform, just moving. Sing in your car. Make sounds. Hum.

These practices reconnect you with emotional expression without requiring you to identify or name what you're feeling.

Art therapy opens doors that words can't. Colors, shapes, and textures can express what's locked inside. You don't need to be "good"—just let your hands create without censoring. Creative projects, role-playing, even simple exercises like making different facial expressions in a mirror, can gradually restart a frozen emotional system. Start gently. Start small. You're thawing ice that's been frozen for a long time.

Practice: Put on music that moves you and allow your body to move intuitively for 15 minutes. Don't try to dance "well," just let your body express whatever wants to come through. Notice any emotions that arise, however subtle. If nothing comes, that's okay too. You're just practicing being present with the possibility of feeling.

SOMATIC PATTERNS

Hyperactive Soma: The Body That Can't Calm Down

Your nervous system is locked in high alert. If this is you, your body never feels safe. Every sound is a potential threat. Every sensation feels amplified. Your heart races for no apparent reason. Your muscles are perpetually tense. Touch feels overwhelming, even painful. Crowded places feel dangerous. Your body is stuck in survival mode, constantly scanning for threats that aren't there.

After surviving an assault, Maria's nervous system stayed in permanent high alert. Every unexpected sound made her jump. Even an affectionate touch from her partner could trigger panic. Her body interpreted every sensation as danger. She couldn't distinguish between excitement and fear because both felt like overwhelming activation.

If this is you, you are not overreacting, and this doesn't need to be permanent. This is a "mode" you can shift out of. Your nervous system experienced something genuinely dangerous and did exactly what it was designed to do—it went into high alert to keep you safe.

The problem is that it never got the signal that the danger passed. Your body is still guarding you against a threat that's no longer there.

How to Heal: You can't force yourself to be calm. Going directly from hyperactivation to stillness usually backfires, creating more tension. Instead, you need to meet your system where it is and then gradually dial it down.

Practice: When feeling activated, put on upbeat music, anything you feel connected to in the moment. Move vigorously—dance, jump, shake—for 15 minutes or until you feel genuinely exhausted. Then gradually slow the music and your movements over the next 10 minutes, ending in stillness. Notice how much more natural the quiet feels when you've honored your system's need to discharge first.

This honors your system's natural rhythms. You're not forcing calm; you're allowing it to emerge naturally after the activation is complete.

A hyperactive Soma can also have biological roots — nutrient deficiencies or excessive stimulants. Never underestimate how much nutrition affects your inner state.

Hypoactive Soma: The Body You Can't Feel

If this is you, you feel like you're floating outside your body rather than inhabiting it. You bump into things. You ignore hunger, pain, and exhaustion signals because you genuinely don't feel them. Your movements feel clumsy and uncoordinated, like you're operating a body you don't quite know how to control.

You might describe feeling "disconnected" or "numb," or like you're "watching yourself from outside." Physical pleasure is difficult to access. You can't tell when you're cold, hungry, or in pain until it becomes extreme.

Following surgery that temporarily paralyzed him, James never fully reconnected with his body, even after physical function returned. He moved through space without awareness, bumping into furniture, ignoring fatigue signals until he collapsed. He couldn't tell when he was hungry or full. His body felt like a distant vehicle he was operating from afar. His sense of where his body was in space was compromised, leaving him feeling ungrounded and perpetually lost.

If this is you, you didn't choose to disconnect from your body. Disconnection was the only way to survive something that felt unbearable. Maybe it was physical pain, maybe trauma, maybe chronic overwhelm. Your nervous system made an executive decision: better to feel nothing than to feel that. It was smart then. But you can come home to your body now, slowly, safely.

How to Heal: You need practices that gently wake up sensation and rebuild the connection between your awareness and your physical experience. Start with pleasure rather than intensity. Warm baths. Gentle massage. Soft textures. You're coaxing your nervous system back online by showing it that physical sensation can feel good.

Movement practices work beautifully but start simple. Gentle stretches where you pay attention to what you feel. Walking while noticing the sensation of your feet touching the ground. Focus on the feeling, not the "doing." The goal is rebuilding the neural pathways between your brain and body that trauma disrupted.

Practice: Lie down and place your hands on your heart. Breathe naturally and imagine your breath flowing to wherever your hands are touching and imagine it being filled with pleasure and light. After a minute, move your hands to your belly and breathe there. Then your shoulders. Your legs. Each area gets 30 seconds of your attention and breath. You're practicing directing connection back into your body, rebuilding the connection one breath at a time.

The beauty of this framework is its simplicity. Healing in every case means supporting your system's return to balance, where all three intelligences function in harmony.

All these techniques, and any healing techniques, require a foundation of safety. If you're in an environment where you don't feel safe, that's always the first step towards healing trauma. Nothing works without it.

You don't need to heal everything at once. Pick one pattern that resonates most strongly. Start with one practice. Ten minutes a day is enough. Perfection doesn't matter, but direction does. Are you moving toward balance?

The Death of Socrates

By 399 BCE, Athens grows tired of Socrates' questions. The city is trying to rebuild after a devastating defeat by Sparta, a paranoid shell of its former self. The citizens want order and stability, not more rebellion. Socrates' method of relentless inquiry is no longer seen as a philosophical curiosity but a threat to the stability of the state.

The charges brought against him were vague: "corrupting the youth" and "introducing new gods." In reality, his "crime" was much simpler. He was demonstrating, in public, that those in power did not know how to lead. They lacked even first principles. The trial is a dramatic saga, immortalized in Plato's book *Apology*. Socrates is given every opportunity to save himself. His friends even grease the palms of guards to arrange an escape into exile. But Socrates refuses. Fleeing would not be an act of courage or virtue. Instead, he chooses to stay and face trial. Inside the prison, the air is heavy with sadness. Socrates remained calm and composed. Plato was there, standing in the shadows with uncontrollable grief, watching his beloved friend and teacher drink poison. As the numbness creeps up his legs, Socrates inquires into the nature of death, wondering aloud if it is a dreamless sleep or maybe a grand opportunity to commune with spirits passed. He uses even his dying moments to continue inquiring and teaching. It is always the acts of great courage that send ripples through time

Sitting in a damp jail cell in Birmingham in 1963, Martin Luther King Jr. wrote, "Academic freedom is a reality today because Socrates practiced civil disobedience. If it had not been for Socrates, academic freedom might never have come to the Western world." In 1990, Steve Jobs claimed he would trade all his Apple stock for an afternoon with Socrates. Einstein, studying in Bern, would credit him as the inspiration for his scientific breakthroughs.

Plato spent the rest of his life writing about Socrates. His dialogues, the academy he founded, and his mentorship of Aristotle were all, in essence, a long, love letter to his dear teacher. Socrates was 70 when he was put to death, and still very vital. I often wonder what the world would be like if Socrates had another 10 or 20 years to live. Had it not been for a few Athenian votes, the Socratic vision might have become the fabric of our social order. We might now be able to discern between principled and unprincipled leaders. We might have built a civilization where the soul and spirituality were the central pursuit. A world where all children were taught to think critically, develop principles for good living, and engage in creating their own version of a virtuous life. A future with living examples everywhere to nurture and support them. And yet, the future is a collective project, and that possibility still exists.

To The Garden

In India, they say the soul's journey happens in three phases, like walking through the woods.

1. **Walking on the path.** You start walking on the path paved for you by your parents and culture. It's safe, there's no need to take risks. However, you slowly begin to notice that there's a vast wilderness beyond the paved path. You get curious, of what happens in the freedom of the untamed woods.

2. **Into the wilderness.** Walking along the path loses its meaning over time. You realize reality is much larger than just a single path, that there are unlimited paths and unlimited possibilities. You're no longer bound. Being off the path is fun and exciting; it's when life begins to open and feel creative. Most people are lucky to get this far. However, exploring the wilderness loses its meaning after a time. It's not the end.

3. **The Garden.** You begin to realize not all parts of the wilderness are pleasant. You begin collecting and

curating the experiences that truly create the life you want. You start building a garden in the woods. You can leave the safety of your garden and return to the wilderness, or the path, when you choose. You have a foundation of safety and the freedom to take risks. You feel a sense of freedom and security, knowing the garden is always there to return to. It's said that very few people make it to the garden

Journal: Kauai

November 2, 2025: Kauai

I wake up and kiss my girlfriend. We sit on the deck and I read the Bible. The sky is clear, and the sun is rising. We talk about faith, then meditate together. I'll propose soon.

I walk along the white-sand beach and listen to an economics podcast. I feel pulls and pains and a little numbness. I stop to do Kundalini yoga. I feel the earth beneath in my feet and the breeze tickling my skin. I'm grateful to be alive.

I work at a cafe and order Matcha. We're preparing to welcome a new cohort of Master's students at Integrative Psych. I feel excitement and a gentle stress. I finish and go to the gym. I read the news on my phone. I call my mom.

It's not the life my parents imagined for me. It's not the life I planned. It's better because it's real and alive. It often feels hard and full of pain. Weeds always grow back. Numbness always needs tending.

Some days I get lost and wander away. But I know how to find my way home. Thinking of all the people who've helped me brings tears.

254

I choose all of it.

Continuing the Journey

The ideas in this book didn't emerge in isolation. They took shape during deep conversations with people all over the world. That conversation doesn't have to end here.

If this book stirred something in you, I'd love to continue our connection. My team at Integrative Psychology runs a free weekly online group support to help people through life challenges and build better mental health. It's a live Zoom session, open to anyone, where we take the ideas in this book and apply them to real life. You can register at **integrativepsychology.org**.

I hope to see you there.

— Adam

Use code: **GURUKOL** for $150 off any of our trainings.

Acknowledgements

I want to thank all of the people who deeply influenced this book, including the late Michael Sugre. His lectures (available on YouTube) were instrumental in deepening my relationship with Greek Philosophy. I also want to thank my co-founder and dear friend Mollie Mendoza, who has been an unwavering support system through this process.

I also want to thank Amri Pal Singh, Deep Kumar, Vijeth Kumar, Susan Bass, Kia Miller, Govind Das, Barrett Tegner, Babaji Harihar Ram, Rudi Cole and Julia Robert, and all those who have been spiritual guides to me.

Bibliography

Ancient Texts & Classical Sources

Homer *The Iliad* and *The Odyssey*. Translated by Robert Fagles. New York: Penguin Classics, 1990 & 1996.

Plato *The Republic*. Translated by G.M.A. Grube, revised by C.D.C. Reeve. Indianapolis: Hackett Publishing, 1992.

The Symposium. Translated by Walter Hamilton. London: Penguin Classics, 1951.

Phaedo. Translated by David Gallop. Oxford: Oxford University Press, 1975.

Apology. Translated by G.M.A. Grube. Indianapolis: Hackett Publishing, 1975.

Phaedrus. Translated by Alexander Nehamas and Paul Woodruff. Indianapolis: Hackett Publishing, 1995.

Diogenes Laertius *Lives of the Eminent Philosophers*. Translated by R.D. Hicks. Cambridge: Harvard University Press (Loeb Classical Library), 1925.

Marcus Aurelius *Meditations*. Translated by Gregory Hays. New York: Modern Library, 2002.

The Yoga Sutras of Patanjali. Translated by Edwin F. Bryant. New York: North Point Press, 2009.

Modern & Contemporary Works

van der Kolk, Bessel A. *The Body Keeps the Score: Brain, Mind, and Body in the Healing of Trauma.* New York: Viking, 2014.

Towards a New Architecture (Vers une architecture). Translated by Frederick Etchells. New York: Dover Publications, 1986. (Originally published 1923.)

Masson, Jeffrey Moussaieff *The Assault on Truth: Freud's Suppression of the Seduction Theory.* New York: Farrar, Straus and Giroux, 1984. *(Referenced as the work that exposed Freud's reversal on patient accounts of childhood abuse, following Masson's access to the Freud Archives.)*

Sacred & Spiritual Texts

The Upanishads Translated by Patrick Olivelle. Oxford: Oxford University Press, 1996. *(Referenced in the context of the phrase "Tat Tvam Asi" — "Thou art That.")*

The Bible (New Testament) *(Referenced throughout, including the Gospel of John and Paul's letters.)*

Historical Figures & Lectures

Mozoomdar, Protap Chunder "The Oriental Christ" and "The Spirit of God in Nature." Lectures delivered in

Boston, ca. 1870s–1880s. *(Quoted directly in the chapter on Vivekananda and the convergence of Hindu and Christian mysticism.)*

Vivekananda, Swami Address at the Parliament of the World's Religions, Chicago, September 11, 1893. *(Referenced in the chapter on Vivekananda's arrival in America.)*

King, Martin Luther, Jr. "Letter from Birmingham Jail," April 16, 1963. *(Quoted directly: "Academic freedom is a reality today because Socrates practiced civil disobedience.")*

Referenced Thinkers (Primary Works Not Directly Quoted but Central to the Narrative)

Freud, Sigmund *The Interpretation of Dreams.* Translated by James Strachey. New York: Basic Books, 1955.

Studies on Hysteria (with Josef Breuer). Translated by James Strachey. New York: Basic Books, 1957.

Janet, Pierre *L'Automatisme Psychologique* (Psychological Automatism). Paris: Alcan, 1889. *(Referenced in the context of "somatic automatisms" and van der Kolk's early research into trauma and the body.)*

Ramakrishna, Sri *The Gospel of Sri Ramakrishna.* Translated by Swami Nikhilananda. New York: Ramakrishna-Vivekananda Center, 1942. *(Referenced in the account of Ramakrishna's meeting with Vivekananda.)*

www.ingramcontent.com/pod-product-compliance
Lightning Source LLC
Chambersburg PA
CBHW030430160726
47991CB00005B/1669